my **revisi⏻n** notes

AS Edexcel History
BRITAIN, c.1860–1930
THE CHANGING POSITION OF WOMEN

Robin Bunce
Laura Gallagher

HODDER
EDUCATION
AN HACHETTE UK COMPANY

The Publishers would like to thank the following for permission to reproduce copyright material:

Photo credits p.29 Cartoon by W.K.Haselden published in *Daily Mirror*, 29 April 1906, British Cartoon Archive, University of Kent © Mirrorpix.

Acknowledgements p.57 Alfred Marshall, private letter, 15 October 1896 from *The Correspondent of Alfred Marshall, Economist*, edited by John K Whitaker (Cambridge University Press, 2005), reproduced by permission of the publisher.

Every effort has been made to trace all copyright holders, but if any have been inadvertently overlooked the Publishers will be pleased to make the necessary arrangements at the first opportunity.

Although every effort has been made to ensure that website addresses are correct at time of going to press, Hodder Education cannot be held responsible for the content of any website mentioned in this book. It is sometimes possible to find a relocated web page by typing in the address of the home page for a website in the URL window of your browser.

Hachette UK's policy is to use papers that are natural, renewable and recyclable products and made from wood grown in sustainable forests. The logging and manufacturing processes are expected to conform to the environmental regulations of the country of origin.

Orders: please contact Bookpoint Ltd, 130 Milton Park, Abingdon, Oxon OX14 4SB. Telephone: +44 (0)1235 827720. Fax: +44 (0)1235 400454. Lines are open 9.00a.m.–5.00p.m., Monday to Saturday, with a 24-hour message answering service. Visit our website at www.hoddereducation.co.uk

© Robin Bunce and Laura Gallagher 2012
First published in 2012 by
Hodder Education,
An Hachette UK Company
338 Euston Road
London NW1 3BH
Impression number   10 9 8 7 6 5 4 3
Year   2016 2015 2014 2013

Cover photo © Mary Evans Picture Library/The Womens Library
Illustrations by Datapage (India) Pvt. Ltd.
Typeset in 11/13 Stempel Schneidler Std by Datapage (India) Pvt. Ltd.
Printed in India
A catalogue record for this title is available from the British Library
ISBN 978 1444 177428

Contents

Introduction

About Unit 2

Unit 2 is worth 50 per cent of your AS level. It requires detailed knowledge of a period of British history and the ability to explore and analyse historical sources. Overall, 60 per cent of the marks available are awarded for source analysis (Assessment Objective 2), and 40 per cent for using own knowledge to form an explanation (Assessment Objective 1).

In the exam, you are required to answer one question with two parts. Part (a) is worth 20 marks and Part (b) is worth 40 marks. It is advisable to spend approximately one-third of your time in the exam on Part (a) and the remaining two-thirds on Part (b). There will be a choice of two Part (b) questions, of which you must answer one.

Part (a) focuses on AO1. It will test your ability to:

■ comprehend source material
■ compare source material in detail, explaining how the sources agree and differ
■ suggest reasons why the sources agree or differ based on their provenance
■ reach an overall judgement.

Part (b) focuses on both AO1 and AO2. It will test your ability to:

■ select information that focuses on the question
■ organise this information to provide an answer to the question
■ integrate information from the sources and own knowledge
■ weigh evidence from sources and own knowledge to reach an overall judgement.

Britain c.1860–1930: The Changing Position of Women and the Suffrage Question

The exam board specifies that students should study four general areas as part of this topic.

1. The changing status of women in the home: marriage, divorce, motherhood, and property rights. The concepts of 'the angel in the house' and 'separate spheres'.

2. The changing political status of women: female involvement in local government, the campaigns of the suffragists and the suffragettes, the First World War and women's suffrage.

3. Political and public responses to the campaigns for women's suffrage: the Liberal Government (1906–1914), the Representation of the People Act (1918), and the Equal Franchise Act (1928).

4. The changing educational and professional status of women: education reforms, workplace reforms, and the impact of the First World War on job opportunities for women.

How to use this book

This book has been designed to help you to develop the knowledge and skills necessary to succeed in this exam. The book is divided into four sections – one for each general area of the course. Each section is made up of a series of topics organised into double-page spreads. On the left-hand page, you will find a summary of the key content you need to learn. Words in bold in the key content are defined in the glossary. On the right-hand page, you will find exam-focused activities. Together, these two strands of the book will take you through the knowledge and skills essential for exam success.

▼ Key historical content   ▼ Exam-focused activities

There are three levels of exam-focused activities:

- Band 1 activities are designed to develop the foundational skills needed to pass the exam. These have a turquoise heading and this symbol:

- Band 2 activities are designed to build on the skills developed in Band 1 activities and to help you achieve a C grade. These have an orange heading and this symbol:

- Band 3 activities are designed to enable you to access the highest grades. These have a purple heading and this symbol:

Some activities have answers or suggested answers on pages 74–76 and have the following symbol to indicate this: **(a)**

Each section ends with an exam-style question and model A grade answer with examiner's commentary. This should give you guidance on what is required to achieve the top grades. You can see the mark scheme on pages 77–78.

You can also keep track of your revision by ticking off each topic heading in the book or by ticking the checklist on the contents page. Tick each box when you have:

- revised and understood a topic
- completed the activities.

Section 1: The changing personal status of women

Amongst the middle classes, the relationship between men and women was underpinned by beliefs about **gender** differences. However, the experience of working-class women was very different.

Middle-class views of women

'Separate spheres'

The philosophy of 'separate spheres' was popular in the early **Victorian period**. This suggested that men and women had very different roles. Men performed their work outside the house, and were expected to earn enough money to support the whole family. In contrast, women were expected to work inside the home, performing **domestic duties** for which they would receive no payment.

The philosophy of 'separate spheres' was based on an understanding of the nature of men and women. It assumed that men were naturally suited to protect the weak, whereas women were naturally vulnerable and in need of protection. Equally, it suggested that men were naturally able to provide, whereas women were dependent on men and unable to provide for themselves.

'Angel in the House'

Related to the 'separate spheres' philosophy was the view that women should be an 'angel in the house'. This assumed that women were naturally good, gentle and weak. The role of a woman was to provide comfort for her husband and children and run her home in a modest, selfless and **godly** way.

Paid work

According to both the 'separate spheres' philosophy and the view that women should be an 'angel in the house', women should not undertake paid work. In the 1860s, working outside the home was considered unladylike, lacking in modesty, and selfish as it prevented women from devoting their full attention to their families. Middle-class women who did work outside the home tended to do characteristically 'feminine' jobs associated with beauty and the arts. For example, in 1861, 168 women were employed as photographers, and 1,618 were employed as musicians.

Sex and marriage

Middle-class attitudes to sex and marriage were based, in part, on the large number of single women in Victorian society. In 1851, 29 per cent of women over the age of twenty were unmarried. By 1861, the problem of 'surplus women' was at its height. Indeed, the 1861 **census** indicated that for every 100 men, there were 143 women. Consequently, many women were unmarried. Amongst middle-class women, competition for men was extremely fierce and female virginity was an essential part of securing a husband.

The fierce competition for men also led to a 'sexual double-standard', whereby male unfaithfulness was easily forgiven but female **infidelity** was unforgiveable. This double-standard was also based on the 'separate spheres' philosophy and the image of the 'angel in the house'. It was believed that men naturally desired sex more than women and that it was against the 'angelic' nature of women to be unfaithful to their husband.

Life for working-class women

Working-class women were not under the same pressure to be 'angels in the home'. Indeed, by 1861, 2.7 million working-class women – one-quarter of the female population – were engaged in paid work. Of this, 2 million were involved in **domestic service** which was low status, poorly paid and involved long hours. Women were also involved in other areas of the economy, for example, 5,500 were employed as miners.

Spot the mistake

Below are a sample exam-style part (a) question and a paragraph written in answer to the question. Why does this paragraph not get into Level 4? Once you have identified the mistake, rewrite the paragraph so that it displays the qualities of Level 4. The mark scheme on page 77 will help you.

Study Sources 1, 2 and 3.

How far do the sources agree that the philosophy of separate spheres implied that women were inferior to men?

> In some ways, the sources agree that the philosophy of separate spheres implied that women were inferior to men. For example, Source 1 suggests that women and men have different skills. The source states that 'Thought is, or ought to be, the characterising feature of man, and feeling the characterising feature of woman.' This implies that women and men occupy different spheres, and that women are inferior because they cannot think as well as men. Source 2 states that neither men nor women are superior. However, it does state that women should not emphasise their equality, suggesting that women should not try to claim equal rights. Although Source 3 states that women have a role of 'amazing responsibility and importance' it also says they should 'dismiss all ambition for anything higher' implying that a woman's sphere is below that of a man. In this way, all three sources agree that that the philosophy of separate spheres implied that women were inferior to men.

SOURCE 1

(Adapted from The Christian Library: Volume 8, *published 1836)*

God has put a difference between the sexes, but education and manners have put a still greater difference. They are designed to move in separate spheres, but occasionally to unite together, in order to soften each other. Thought is, or ought to be, the characterising feature of man, and feeling the characterising feature of the woman.

SOURCE 2

(Adapted from Mary Tucker Magill, Women, or, Chronicles of the Late War, *published 1871)*

It is impossible to assert the superiority of either man or woman, because their separate spheres are so different. That man is a fool who is continually referring to the inferiority of the opposite sex. And the woman is worse who is always asserting either her equality or her superiority to the man.

SOURCE 3

(From John Milton Williams, Woman Suffrage, *published 1893)*

Woman has no to call the ballot-box, but she has a sphere of her own, of amazing responsibility and importance. She is the divinely appointed guardian of the home. She should more fully realise that her position is the holiest, most responsible, and queenlike assigned to mortals, and dismiss all ambition for anything higher, as there is nothing else here so high for mortals.

 Linking sources

Above is a sample part (a) question and the three sources referred to in the question. In one colour, draw links between the sources to show ways in which they agree that the philosophy of separate spheres implied that women were inferior to men. In another colour, draw links between the sources to show ways in which they disagree that the philosophy of separate spheres implied that women were inferior to men.

Early legal reforms

In the early nineteenth century, a married woman had no legal status independent of her husband. Therefore, when a woman got married, ownership of her property and income was transferred to her husband. Equally, a wife had no legal rights over her children.

Women were often trapped in unhappy marriages. Divorce was extremely difficult to obtain, and could only be granted by an Act of Parliament.

Legal changes to the status of women

As a result of Caroline Norton's campaign, there was a series of changes to women's rights as shown in the table below.

The case of Caroline Norton

The writer Caroline Sheridan married George Norton in 1827. After years of misery, including regular beatings, Caroline left her husband. George retaliated by sending their three children to Scotland and by confiscating Caroline's earnings. He refused to allow her to apply for a divorce.

Caroline began a campaign to change the legal status of women. She wrote two pamphlets: 'The Natural Claim of a Mother to the Custody of her Children' (1837) and 'English Laws of Women' (1854).

Law	Date	Provision	Limitations
Custody of Children Act	1839	A wife was entitled to the custody of children under seven if the **Lord Chancellor** agreed that she was of 'good character'.	• Women could not gain custody of children over seven. • The law assumed that custody of children was the husband's right unless a wife protested.

Divorce and Matrimonial Causes Act	1857	Reforms to divorce:
		• Divorce could be granted by a court rather than by Parliament. This reduced the cost of obtaining a divorce, making divorce accessible to less wealthy families.
		• A husband could obtain a divorce if he could prove his wife had committed adultery.
		• A wife could only obtain a divorce if she could prove her husband had committed adultery and one of the following acts:
		  – **Bigamy**
		  – Rape
		  – **Sodomy**
		  – **Bestiality**
		  – Cruelty
		  – Long-term **desertion** (a minimum of two years).
		The right to separation:
		• A decree of separation could be granted in court cases where a husband was guilty of adultery, cruelty, or long-term desertion. In this sense, it was easier for women to obtain a separation than a divorce.
		Women's rights following divorce or separation:
		• Wives could keep their own income.
		• Courts could order husbands to pay maintenance payments to their wives.
		• Wives had the same rights as single women to inherit and make wills.
		• Wives could take someone to court or be taken to court independently of their husbands.
			• The law gave no new rights to wives who continued to live with their husbands.
			• It continued a double-standard in divorce laws: husbands could divorce their wives for adultery alone, whereas wives had to prove that their husbands had committed adultery plus another immoral act.

Separation and divorce

Separation referred to the legal recognition that a husband and wife were no longer living together. Separation did not permit either party to remarry. However, it did allow women to claim the rights set out in the 1857 Act.

Mind map

Use the information on the opposite page to add detail to the mind map below.

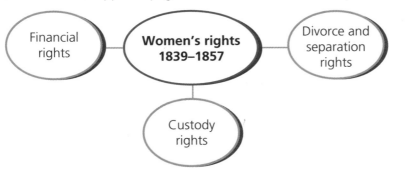

Financial rights — **Women's rights 1839–1857** — Divorce and separation rights — Custody rights

Add own knowledge

Below are a sample part (b) question and the three sources referred to in the question. In one colour, draw links between the sources to show ways in which they agree about the extent to which the Divorce and Matrimonial Causes Act of 1857 was a significant step towards sexual equality in Britain. In another colour, draw links between the sources to show ways in which they disagree. Around the edge of the sources, write relevant own knowledge. Again, draw links to show the ways in which this agrees and disagrees with the sources.

Use Sources 1, 2 and 3 and your own knowledge.

Do you agree with the view that the Divorce and Matrimonial Causes Act of 1857 was a significant step towards sexual equality in Britain?

SOURCE 1

(From The Leeds Mercury, *2 December 1856. The article is discussing the proposed Matrimonial Causes Act)*

It is well known to our readers that as matters stand at present, while the rich husband can procure an absolute divorce from his unfaithful wife with full liberty to marry again, no such relief is afforded to the poor man, or to the wife, whether rich or poor.

SOURCE 2

(Adapted from Nicola Diane Thompson, Victorian Women Writers and the Woman Question, *published 1999)*

The Matrimonial Causes Act was quite conservative, not touching the double-standard or traditional male-dominated structures, but it did increase the availability of both legal separation and full divorce for the middle classes and for women, and increasing numbers of both groups took advantage of it after 1857. There were a couple of important new provisions in the 1857 Act – one, the protection of judicially separated women's property, and two, the addition of cruelty and desertion for two years to the causes for divorce for women.

SOURCE 3

(From Paula Bartley, Votes for Women, *published 2007)*

The 1857 Divorce Act reformed the divorce law, but it benefited men rather than women. This, argued nineteenth-century feminists, consolidated the sexual double-standard because it laid down different grounds for divorce. Moreover, once divorced, women found it difficult to obtain maintenance and custody of their children.

The legal status of marriage, 1873–1895

Between 1873 and 1895 a series of legal reforms transformed women's rights:

Date	Reform	Key features
1873	Custody of Infants Act	Courts could award custody of children under the age of sixteen to the mother.
1878	Matrimonial Causes Act	In cases of assault on the part of the husband, local magistrates could order: • The legal separation of the couple. • Maintenance payments from the husband to the wife. • Police protection of the wife to prevent further attacks.
1884	Matrimonial Causes Act	• Husbands were prohibited from locking up their wives for refusing to have sex. Significantly, however, rape within marriage was not outlawed. • A spouse deserted by their partner could ask for an immediate divorce or separation. • Husbands or wives could no longer be imprisoned for refusing to live with their partners.
1886	Maintenance of Wives Act	Magistrates could enforce (rather than just order) maintenance payments of up to £2 per week.
1886	Guardianship of Infants Act	Custody of children was decided on the basis of the child's welfare.
1895	Summary Jurisdiction Act (Married Women Act)	Immediate divorces were permitted in cases where the wife had been assaulted, the husband had deserted the wife, the wife had been forced from her home, or there was evidence of persistent cruelty.

The impact of the Acts

Divorce and separation rates

By 1899, two of every thousand marriages ended in divorce, whereas 38 couples per thousand separated. The difference can be explained by the following:

- A divorce cost the equivalent of 30 weeks' wages for a working man.
- Divorce courts were located in London alone. In contrast, after 1878, separations could be granted by local magistrates.
- For women, the criteria for gaining a divorce were much stricter than those for gaining a separation. Consequently, women wishing to leave their husbands were ten times more likely to apply for a separation than a divorce.
- Divorce was viewed as more shameful than separation due to the fact that divorce cases were reported in great detail in newspapers.

The inequalities contained in nineteenth-century divorce legislation were noted by the 1909 Royal Commission on Divorce. The Commission recommended that divorce be equally accessible to rich and poor, and that the criteria for seeking a divorce should be the same for men and women. However, no immediate action was taken to address these issues.

Marital violence

Magistrates were often unwilling to uphold the rights of assaulted wives. For example, in Preston in 1879, the Police Court granted separation orders to only four of 55 women who provided proof of assault.

However, statistical evidence indicates that the Matrimonial Causes Acts did lead to a decrease in marital violence. For example, in London in 1883, there were 800 recorded cases of wife-beating. This figure had fallen to 200 by 1889.

Custody of children

Determining what was meant by 'the welfare of the child' in the 1886 Guardianship of Infants Act was difficult. In some cases, custody was awarded on religious grounds, as the court believed that a Protestant upbringing was superior to that of another religion.

Spot the inference

High level answers avoid summarising or paraphrasing the sources, and instead make inferences from the sources. On the right is a source and below is a series of statements. Read Source 1 and decide which of the statements:

- make inferences from the source (I)
- summarise the source (S)
- paraphrase the source (P)
- cannot be justified from the source (X).

Statement	I	P	S	X
Following the 1878 Matrimonial Causes Act, separations were rare and in many cases beaten women found it hard to obtain a separation.				
The Matrimonial Causes Act of 1878 failed to bring about substantial change for women.				
Between 1878 and 1893, it was extremely rare for judges to issue separation orders.				
The 1878 Matrimonial Causes Act brought about sexual equality for women.				
Judges were reluctant to enforce the terms of the 1878 Matrimonial Causes Act.				

 Eliminate irrelevance

Below are a sample exam-style part (b) question and a paragraph written in answer to this question. The question refers to Source 1 above, and Sources 2 and 3 below. Read the paragraph and identify parts of the paragraph that are not directly relevant to the question. Draw a line through the information that is irrelevant and justify your deletions in the margin.

Use Sources 1, 2 and 3 and your own knowledge.

Do you agree with the view that there was a revolution in the legal status of women between 1873 and 1895?

There is evidence in all three sources to suggest that legislation between 1873 and 1895 did create a significant change in the legal status of women. Source 3, in reference to the Guardianship of Infants Act of 1886, notes that 'the custom in divorce cases was for custody to go to the innocent parent' suggesting that following divorce mothers and fathers were assessed equally for custody. This source was written by Claudia Nelson in 2007 so she was not around at the time she describes. Indeed, the Guardianship of Infants Act specifically stated that custody would be granted on the basis of the child's welfare and therefore not according to the gender of the parents. Equally, Source 2 provides an example of a woman being awarded maintenance payments following the 1886 Maintenance of Wives Act. The husband, named Ellis, objected saying that 'his wife had sold his furniture and had really deserted him.' Indeed, the Act stated that wives could receive a maintenance payment of up to £2 per week. In this way, the 1886 Acts clearly improved the status of women because they gave women new legal rights following divorce and separation.

SOURCE 3

(Adapted from Claudia Nelson, Family Ties in Victorian England, published 2007)

After the passage of the Guardianship of Infants Act of 1886, the custom in divorce cases was for custody to go to the innocent parent. In general, women who had been found unfaithful to their husbands had little chance of retaining their children. The stereotype of the sexual purity of the good mother was so powerful that mothers who failed to live up to it were not considered mothers at all.

SOURCE 1

(Adapted from Mary Lyndon Shanley, Feminism, Marriage, and the Law in Victorian England, published 1993)

In 1893, Mabel Sharman Crawford looked back over the fourteen years in which the Matrimonial Causes Act of 1878 had been in operation and claimed that it was 'a rare event' for magistrates' courts to issue a separation order. She gave accounts of literally dozens of cases that were disposed of during a six-week period in 1892. In one a man deliberately set fire to his wife, and in another a pregnant wife was 'kicked, and dragged upstairs by the hair, thrown down and jumped upon by both feet, almost strangled by a cord.' In this case the husband was sentenced to two months' imprisonment, and no separation order was granted.

SOURCE 2

(Adapted from The Manchester Evening News, 15 July 1886)

One of the first cases in the country heard under the Maintenance of Wives Act, which came into operation at the end of last month, was heard at Sheffield today, when a man named Ellis was summoned for deserting his wife. He stated that his wife had sold his furniture and had really deserted him. The magistrates ordered him to pay 5s a week.

Two significant marriage cases

Revised

Both the Weldon Case of 1883 and the Jackson Case of 1891 concerned the extent to which a husband or wife had the right to claim **conjugal rights**.

The Weldon Case, 1883

The Weldon Case concerned the marriage of Harry and Georgina Weldon. The Weldons had separated in 1875, with Harry providing Georgina with £1000 a year and a large house. In 1878, in an attempt to avoid these payments, Harry had his wife committed to a lunatic asylum. Georgina escaped, and sued her husband for a restoration of conjugal rights. She won the case, and the court ruled that the couple must live together. Harry refused and was sent to gaol – he stated that he would rather be imprisoned than live with his wife.

The Weldon Case led to a change in the legal duty of spouses to respect each other's conjugal rights. Parliament was moved by the case of Harry Weldon and introduced the 1884 Matrimonial Causes Act (see page 8) which ended the courts' power to imprison husbands or wives who refused to live with their partners.

The Jackson Marriage Case, 1891

The Jackson Marriage Case (or Clitheroe Case) concerned the marriage of Edmund and Emily Jackson. Five days after their marriage, Edmund moved to New Zealand, intending Emily to join him. However, in his absence, Emily went back to her family.

On his return, Edmund sought a restoration of conjugal rights. When persuasion failed, he kidnapped Emily and imprisoned her in his home, placing her under the care of his sister and a doctor. Emily's family responded by **picketing** the house and Edmund employed a band of men to prevent Emily's escape.

Emily's family went to court to seek her release. The court ruled that her imprisonment was legitimate due to the fact that a husband had the right to lock up his wife as long as he did not harm her. Emily's family appealed and the Appeal Court ruled that Edmund had no right to lock up his wife. Consequently, Emily was released.

Reactions to the Jackson Case

The Appeal Court ruling was controversial. Emily's family home in Clitheroe was stoned by local residents. Additionally, *The Times* newspaper claimed that 'marriage in England was abolished' by the Appeal Court ruling.

However, *The Times* Law Report argued that the ruling was 'a **charter** of the personal liberty of the married woman'. In this sense, it argued that the Case was a huge step forward for women's rights in Britain. Clearly, the ruling restricted a husband's right to demand cohabitation with his wife.

Divorce, separation and perceptions of women

In some ways, the new divorce and separation rights gained by women between 1857 and 1891 supported traditional interpretations of a woman's role. For example, the right to divorce, legal separation and maintenance were only granted to women who had remained faithful to their husbands and had acted as 'angels in the house'. Equally, rights to custody were consistent with the belief that women and men operated in 'separate spheres' (see page 4), where the woman's role involved nurturing. Nonetheless, these changes were the first legal recognition of the rights of women within marriage.

The following sources give different accounts of the Jackson Marriage Case. List the ways in which the sources differ. Explain the differences between the sources using the provenance of the sources alone. The provenance appears at the top of the source in brackets.

SOURCE 1

(Adapted from part of an anonymous letter to the Editor from a male reader of the North-Eastern Daily Gazette, *21 March 1891)*

Sir – A great deal has been written upon this notable case from Mrs Jackson's point of view, but I have not yet seen any arguments advanced on the other side. I think there is much to be said from the husband's standpoint and that on the whole Mr Jackson is a very ill-used man. In the case in question there is no allegation of any improper means being used to force a marriage. Mrs Jackson entered into marriage of her own free will, not as a young and inexperienced girl but as a woman of middle life.

The highest court of the land has held that the solemn contract which a bride enters into throws not a single legal obligation on her. She can viciously ruin a man's life. I venture to suggest that the decision [in the Jackson Marriage Case] strikes a severe blow to the sacredness of marriage.

SOURCE 2

(Adapted from an interview with Mrs Jackson, published in The Manchester Times, *20 March 1891. At the time of the interview, Mrs Jackson was being held captive by her husband)*

Mrs Jackson said she did not now feel any ill effects from her forcible removal of last Sunday. She stated 'Mr Jackson has certainly been most kind and considerate to me, and I have not complained to him or anyone. Still I am hopeful that before long I may be able to resume my quiet and happy mode of life.' She said she had no idea as to what might be the future action of her husband, but she did not think he had any desire to be harsh with her or do anything against her wish.

The sources on this page relate to the Jackson Marriage Case. Read the information on the opposite page about the Case. Having done this, write an exam-style part (a) question using Sources 1 and 2 above, and Source 3 below.

Study Sources 1, 2 and 3.

How far do the sources agree that...

_____

_____

SOURCE 3

(Adapted from The Leeds Mercury, *20 March 1891)*

The law is that the husband has no right to imprison his wife. The theory that the wife is the property of the husband, to be dealt with as he pleases, is no part of the law of this country. The notion that every true Briton is entitled to beat his wife has long been discredited.

Married women and property reform, 1870–1882

Most of the Acts relating to women passed in the late Victorian period extended women's rights in situations where their marriages were breaking down. By contrast, the Married Women's Property Acts of 1870 and 1882 extended the rights of women within marriage.

Marriage and property prior to 1870

Prior to 1870, marriage significantly changed the legal and financial status of a woman. On marriage, all of a wife's property became that of her husband, and after marriage all of a wife's earnings belonged to her husband. Additionally, a married woman could not make a will.

Property and unmarried women

In contrast to married women, unmarried women were recognised by the law as financially independent. They could own and inherit property, they had control of any income they earned, they were liable for debt, and could make a will.

Reasons for reform

High profile cases such as the Norton Case (see page 6) showed the public that the legal position of women needed reform. Women such as **Barbara Leigh Smith** began organising a campaign for legal change. She sent a petition of 260,000 signatures to Parliament demanding equal property rights for women. Some radical men, such as **John Stuart Mill**, and the leaders of the **Law Amendment Society** supported her campaign. They argued that women were being treated like criminals, children, or the insane – the only other groups forced to surrender property. Finally, many **Liberal** MPs were prepared to compromise on women's property rights in an attempt to diffuse the campaign for women's **suffrage**.

The Married Women's Property Act, 1870

The terms of the Act

The Married Women's Property Act of 1870 gave women marrying after 1870 additional legal rights. They could:

- inherit property, and money up to £200
- inherit rental property
- retain possession of their earnings from work and investments after marriage. However, income generated before marriage remained the property of the husband.

The limitations of the Act

The Act did not affect property already transferred from a wife to her husband prior to 1870. Therefore, property and money already transferred to a husband remained his possession. In addition, the limit of £200 helped working-class and lower-middle-class women, but was of little benefit to wealthier women who would otherwise have inherited much larger sums of money.

The Married Woman's Property Act, 1882

The Married Women's Property Act of 1882 gave married women the same property rights as single women. They could:

- inherit unlimited property and money
- take people to court and be taken to court
- take responsibility for their own debts.

Therefore, married women became recognised as legally distinct from their husbands.

The impact of the Property Acts

According to historian Jennifer Phegley, 'The 1882 law … came the closest of any marriage reforms of the century to allowing the existence of marriages in which both partners were equal under the law.' However, legal equality did not guarantee full equality. Few married women were employed, and those that were employed were restricted to low-paid jobs. Therefore, the right to an income benefited very few married women.

Support or challenge?

Below is a sample part (a) exam-style question which asks you how far the sources agree with a specific statement. Below this are two sources which give information relevant to the question. Identify whether the sources support, mainly support, mainly challenge, or challenge the statement in the question and then give reasons for your answer.

Study Sources 1 and 2.

How far do the sources suggest that the Married Women's Property Acts of 1870 and 1882 failed to protect the rights of women?

SOURCE 1

(*Adapted from* The Manchester Evening News, *24 January 1879*)

The annual meeting of the Married Women's Property Committee was held yesterday afternoon in London. Mr Jacob Bright, MP, chairman, spoke of the unsatisfactory state of the law under the Married Woman's Property Act. He mentioned the case of a man who, being legally separated from his wife, had returned to her home and robbed her, and, according to the decision of the magistrate, the woman could not appeal to the law.

This *source supports / mainly supports / mainly challenges / challenges* the view that the Married Women's Property Acts of 1870 and 1882 failed to protect the rights of women because

_____

_____

SOURCE 2

(*Adapted from the* Portsmouth Evening News, *2 January 1883*)

A wife applied to the magistrate and said that her husband left her a month ago. She wished for protection under the Married Women's Property Act. The magistrate said it would not be right to grant this in such a case. He could not, unless the husband beat her. The wife left the court evidently dissatisfied.

This *source supports / mainly supports / mainly challenges / challenges* the view that the Married Women's Property Acts of 1870 and 1882 failed to protect the rights of women because

_____

_____

 RAG – Rate the line

Below are a sample exam-style part (b) question and a timeline. Read the question, study the timeline and, using three coloured pens, put a red, amber or green star next to the events to show:

- **Red:** Events and policies that have no relevance to the question
- **Amber:** Events and policies that have some significance to the question
- **Green:** Events and policies that are directly relevant to the question

Do you agree with the view that legal change during the Victorian period challenged the notion of separate spheres?

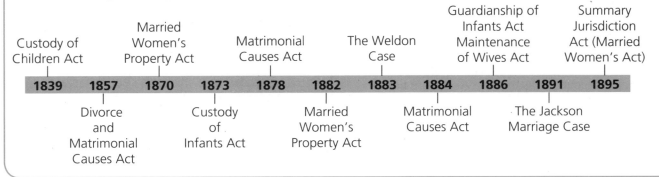

Josephine Butler and the Contagious Diseases Acts, 1864–1885

The Contagious Diseases Acts of 1864–1869 were intended to stop the spread of sexually transmitted diseases in the armed forces.

Date of the Contagious Disease Act	Provisions
1864	• Gave authorities in **naval towns**, and some **garrison towns**, the right to arrest women suspected of being **prostitutes** and subject them to a **gynaecological** examination.
1866	• Extended the 1864 Act to give authorities the power to arrest and examine women within a ten-mile radius of naval ports and some garrison towns. • Within this radius, women suspected of being prostitutes were required to submit to a gynaecological examination every three months.
1869	• Extended the 1866 Act to cover all garrison towns. • Women suspected of being prostitutes could be imprisoned for five days prior to examination.

Objections to the Acts

Many objected to the Acts for the following reasons:

- They gave the government a high degree of power over a woman's body.
- The Acts placed the blame for the spread of sexually transmitted diseases on female prostitutes rather than their male customers.
- Many women who were not prostitutes were arrested and examined.
- The shame of examinations sometimes led to women losing their jobs or even committing suicide.
- The examinations were not always held in private. For example, at the Devonport Dock Yard, male dock workers could observe the examination through a window.

Widespread objections were raised to a proposal to extend the 1869 Act to cover women suspected of prostitution throughout the country.

Josephine Butler and the campaign against the Contagious Diseases Acts

In 1869, **Josephine Butler** created the Ladies National Association for the Repeal of the Contagious Diseases Acts. The Association was led by a group of middle-class women with political contacts. In 1870, they published a **manifesto** signed by 140 well-known women, including **Florence Nightingale**. Their main objection was that the Acts were based on a sexual double-standard: they punished women for sex outside marriage, but did nothing to stop men exploiting women and even young girls.

The Ladies National Association campaigned by sending letters and co-ordinating rallies. By 1871, the Association had 57 branches across the country, and had organised 17,367 petitions signed by over 2.6 million people. Their most effective tactic was campaigning for the replacement of **Parliamentary candidates** who supported the existing laws.

The impact of the campaigns

The Ladies National Association was not the only group campaigning against the Acts:

- In 1875, the **National Medical Association** was founded to campaign against the Acts.
- The same year, the Working Men's National League was created to encourage working men to call for the **repeal** of the Acts.
- In 1883, 72 MPs expressed their disapproval of the Acts in the House of Parliament.

The campaign was very successful. In 1886, the Contagious Diseases Acts were repealed. Furthermore, the **age of consent** was increased from thirteen to sixteen, preventing the exploitation of young girls.

Josephine Butler and the 'Angel in the House'

Notably, Josephine Butler did little to challenge existing stereotypes of women. She presented prostitutes as vulnerable women exploited by ruthless men, and argued that women were naturally virtuous and caring. In this sense Butler supported, rather than challenged, the image of the 'angel in the house'.

Doing reliability well

Below are a series of definitions listing common reasons why sources are either reliable or unreliable, and two sources. Under each source, explain why the source is either reliable or unreliable for the purpose stated, justifying your answer by referring to the following definitions.

- **Vested interest:** the source is written so that the writer can protect their power or their financial interests.
- **Second-hand report:** the writer of the source is not an eyewitness, but is relying on someone else's account.
- **Expertise:** the source is written on a subject which the author (for example a historian) is an expert.
- **Political bias:** a source is written by some with strong political views and reflects these views.
- **Reputation:** a source is written to protect the writer's reputation.

SOURCE 1

(From The Shield, *25 July 1870. The Shield was the weekly publication produced by the Ladies National Association for the Repeal of the Contagious Diseases Acts)*

The system of these acts *is* a conspiracy, of the foulest kind, against the womanhood of the realm ... We do not wonder, for a moment, at the promoters of it using every means to keep it from general knowledge.

The source is <u>reliable / fairly reliable / fairly unreliable / unreliable</u> as evidence of public feelings about the Contagious Diseases Acts in 1870 because

_____

_____

SOURCE 2

(From Josephine Butler, Personal Reminiscences of a Great Crusade, *published 1910)*

From there I went (January 1870) to Leeds, Newcastle, Sunderland, Darlington, and other places, and shortly afterwards a series of visits was paid to Birmingham and other towns of the Midland district. Everywhere the working men organised meetings [against the Contagious Diseases Acts], writing or telegraphing in advance to friends and acquaintances. The meetings were followed by prompt organisation for action, headed in most cases by leading working men.

The source is <u>reliable / fairly reliable / fairly unreliable / unreliable</u> as evidence of public feelings about the Contagious Diseases Acts in 1870 because

_____

_____

 Recommended reading

Below is a list of suggested further reading on this topic.

- Barbara Caine, *Victorian Feminists*, pages 43–53 (1993)
- Malcolm Pearce and Geoffrey Stewart, *British Political History 1867–1900,* pages 14–16 (1992)
- Susan Kingsley Kent, *Sex and Suffrage in Britain 1860–1914*, pages 60–79 (1990)

Exam focus

On pages 17–19 are sample answers to the exam-style questions on this page. Read the answers and the examiner comments around them.

(a) Study Sources 1, 2 and 3.

How far do Sources 2 and 3 challenge the view presented in Source 1 about the Contagious Diseases Acts? Explain your answer, using the evidence of Sources 1, 2 and 3. **(20 marks)**

(b) Use Sources 4, 5 and 6 and your own knowledge.

Do you agree with the view that changes to the laws relating to marriage in the period 1860–1900 challenged the idea that men and women should occupy 'separate spheres'?

Explain your answer, using Sources 4, 5 and 6 and your own knowledge. **(40 marks)**

SOURCE 1

(Adapted from a report of a meeting of the Scotland Free Church General Assembly, 1871)

The [Contagious Diseases] Acts appear to us to be calculated to inflict much bodily and mental suffering on a very helpless class of the community, to outrage their feelings, and to infringe upon their right to be protected against indecent examination, while their effectiveness for the purpose they were introduced is, to say the least, extremely doubtful.

SOURCE 2

(Adapted from Lyon Playfair, Motion for the Repeal of the Contagious Diseases Acts, 1870. Dr Playfair is arguing in favour of keeping the Acts)

The injustice [of the Contagious Diseases Acts] is said to rest in the fact that they apply restrictions to women which they do not apply to men, although both are equally responsible for the spread of disease. However, to discuss the question of who is most responsible for the spread of disease is as pointless as debating which side of a pair of scissors was most useful in cutting.

The law regulates all trades which are liable to abuse and in doing so looks to the vendor only, although the purchaser is equally necessary for trade. The fact that women only are the subject of these Acts arises from the fact that they alone are traders in this form of vice.

SOURCE 3

(From an interview with a prostitute conducted by Josephine Butler in 1870. The interviewee is describing the impact of the Contagious Diseases Acts)

It is *men men men*, from the first to the last that we have to do with! To please a man I did wrong at first, then I was flung about from man to man, then men police lay hands on us – by men we are examined, handled, doctored and messed on with. We are had up before Magistrates who are men, and we never get out of the hands of men till we die!

SOURCE 4

(Adapted from Ben Griffin, The Politics of Gender in Victorian Britain, *published 2012)*

The Guardianship of Infants Act was a very limited measure. As with the Married Women's Property Acts we see that politicians were prepared to make changes to women's legal rights because they did not expect these changes substantially to undermine male domestic authority.

SOURCE 5

(Adapted from Mary Lyndon Shanley, Feminism, Marriage and the Law in Victorian England, *published 1993)*

The Married Women's Property Act of 1882 gave a woman control over any money she brought into a marriage, but the number of middle-class women bringing money into a marriage was not large, and even the most passionate campaigners for women's rights did not suggest that middle-class women should go out to work.

SOURCE 6

(From a speech made by a member of the House of Lords during a Parliamentary debate in 1870. The speech was given in opposition to the Married Women's Property Bill which became law in 1870)

The Married Women's Property Bill is, in fact, an entire subversion of the system of domestic rule which had prevailed in this country for more than 1,000 years. Under this provision a woman might receive a legacy of £20,000. The husband, perhaps, would suggest that the legacy should benefit the children, but she would answer—'At present I have set my heart on a beautiful diamond necklace.' Thus the money would be wasted.

(a) Study Sources 1, 2 and 3.

How far do Sources 2 and 3 challenge the view presented in Source 1 about the Contagious Diseases Acts? Explain your answer, using the evidence of Sources 1, 2 and 3. **(20 marks)**

Source 1 argues that the Contagious Diseases Acts were designed to harm women, to offend their feelings, ignore their rights. In addition, the source argues that the Acts were ineffective in preventing the spread of disease. In general, Source 3 supports this argument, whereas Source 2 contradicts it.

Source 3 clearly agrees with Source 1 that the Contagious Diseases Acts led to 'outrage' amongst women. Source 3's tone clearly implies outrage. For example, it begins 'men, men, men, from the first to the last that we have to do with!'. Source 3 also agrees with Source 1 that the Contagious Diseases Acts infringed women's 'right to be protected against indecent examination'. The prostitute in Source 3 claims she has been 'examined, handled, doctored and messed on with.' Source 2 supports Source 1 to some extent as Source 1 argues that the Contagious Diseases Acts affect 'a very helpless class of the community', meaning women, and Source 2 acknowledges that the Act applies only to women. Source 3's account of the nature of the Contagious Diseases Acts can be trusted because it is a first-hand account of a prostitute who had been examined under the terms of the Acts. However, the prostitute was interviewed by Josephine Butler, the leading campaigner against the Contagious Diseases Acts, and therefore Butler may have been selective in her account of the conversation.

Source 2 clearly disagrees with the account of the Contagious Diseases Acts given in Source 1. Source 1 argues that the Acts were 'calculated to inflict much bodily and mental suffering' on women. However, Source 2 argues that the Acts were not designed to persecute women. Rather, it argues that women are examined because 'they alone are traders in this form of vice.' In this sense, he argues that it is the same as any other law dealing with people who sell services. Additionally, Source 2 suggests that the Acts are necessary to stop the 'spread of disease'. However, Source 1 argues that the Acts' 'effectiveness for the purpose they were introduced is, to say the least, extremely doubtful.' Source 2 gives a very different account to Source 1 and Source 3 because Source 2 is defending the theory behind the Acts, whereas Source 1 and Source 3 are discussing the consequences of the Acts for the lives of women.

In conclusion, Source 3 agrees with the view presented in Source 1 that the Contagious Diseases Acts were harmful to women. Source 2, however, disagrees with Source 1, as it claims the Acts do not reflect any intention to harm women. Additionally, Source 2 contradicts Source 1 as it suggests that the Acts are effective, whereas Source 1 argues that they are not.

This is a focused introduction that analyses the opinion of Source 1 and sets out the positions of Source 2 and Source 3 in relation to this.

The essay makes effective use of quotations from the sources to support the points that are made.

The similarities between the three sources are clearly drawn out and the reliability of Source 3 is analysed based on its provenance.

This paragraph explains the differences between Source 2 and Sources 1 and 3, with reference to the purpose and nature of the Sources.

20/20

The essay on page 17 has a strong focus on the question and thorough cross-referencing of the arguments presented by the sources. The response is well structured and takes into account the provenance and nature of the sources in order to explain why the sources disagree on the nature of the Contagious Diseases Acts.

(b) Use Sources 4, 5 and 6 and your own knowledge.

Do you agree with the view that changes to the laws relating to marriage in the period 1860–1900 challenged the idea that men and women should occupy 'separate spheres'?

Explain your answer, using Sources 4, 5 and 6 and your own knowledge. **(40 marks)**

'Separate spheres' implied that men and women had distinct roles within marriage. The man's sphere related to money, property, and the role of providing for his wife and children. The woman's sphere related to domestic duties, working inside the home. Significantly, 'separate spheres' implied that the woman was dependent on her husband for financial provision and that the husband was the legal representative of the whole family.

Changes in the laws relating to marriage in the period 1860–1900 did not fundamentally challenge the idea that men and women should occupy 'separate spheres'. Nonetheless, they were a step away from total dependence of women on men and therefore a step towards a more independent life for married women. Sources 4 and 5, both written by modern historians, are clear that measures such as the Married Women's Property Act were very limited in their impact on the idea of 'separate spheres'. However, Source 6, a speech by a member of the House of Lords, describes them as a 'subversion of the system of domestic rule' indicating that, at the time, these limited reforms were viewed as a radical change.

Clearly, there is some evidence that legal reforms in the period 1860–1900 did undermine the idea of 'separate spheres'. Source 6 argues that the Married Women's Property Bill, which became law in 1870, would end the husband's dominance, a feature of domestic life 'in this country for more than a thousand years.' Source 6 argues that it will lead to the end of a husband's right to stop his wife spending money badly. Indeed, the Married Women's Property Act did give women three important legal rights. They could inherit property, and money up to a value of £200, they could inherit rented property, and they could legally keep anything they earned during their marriage. Furthermore, Source 5 argues that 'The Married Women's Property Act of 1882 gave a woman control over any money she brought into the marriage.' Indeed, it went further by allowing women to inherit unlimited property and money and to take people to court. In this sense, for the first time, women were legally distinct from their husbands. Women gained further rights due to the Matrimonial Causes Acts of 1878 and 1886, which allowed women to separate from their husbands. Additionally, there were reforms to women's rights over their children, with the 1886 Guardianship of Infants Act formally giving the courts the right to award custody based on the welfare of the child, rather than the rights of the husband. In this way, legislation between 1860 and 1900 did challenge the philosophy of 'separate spheres' in a small way by emphasising a wife's legal and financial independence from her husband.

The essay begins with a clear definition of the key term in the question, 'separate spheres'.

The first line of this paragraph provides a clear answer to the question.

This introductory paragraph contrasts all three of the sources, drawing links to the question. This shows that the candidate is focusing on both the sources and the question.

The sources are used early in the paragraph and quickly linked to own knowledge.

The essay introduces detailed own knowledge of relevant legislation.

In contrast, Sources 4 and 5 indicate that legal change in the period 1860–1900 represented only limited change to the roles of men and women. Source 4, for example, argues that legal changes were only made on the understanding that law makers 'did not expect these changes ... to undermine male domestic authority.' Source 5 supports this, noting that the impact of the Married Women's Property Act of 1882 'was not large' and only affected a small number of middle-class women. In practice, legal reforms did little to undermine traditional views of a woman's role. Many reforms emphasised the woman's role as mother within a family. For example, the Custody of Infants Act of 1873 and the Guardianship of Infants Act of 1886 merely recognised a woman's right to be a mother and therefore did nothing to challenge the idea that a woman's sphere was domestic. Equally, the Maintenance of Wives Act of 1886 emphasised a woman's financial dependence on her husband, even after the marriage had ended. Furthermore, as Source 5 indicates, much of the legal reform recognised that women might bring money into the marriage, but 'did not suggest that middle-class women should go out to work' once married. In this way, legal reform in the period 1860–1900 was not the 'subversion of the system of domestic rule' that Source 6 suggests it was, rather it represented a small change to women's legal rights, which were still rooted in the philosophy of 'separate spheres'.

In conclusion, Source 6 is wrong to suggest that nineteenth-century legal reform to marriage was a revolution in the role of women. It may have seemed this way to the writer of Source 6, a member of the House of Lords, but this indicates just how conservative many of the people making laws were during this period. In actual fact, Victorian legal reform merely gave women more rights within their existing sphere. The one exception is the 1882 Married Women's Property Act which for the first time allowed married women to go to court in their own right. This was a significant step forward which recognised a woman's legal independence and therefore subtly undermined the philosophy of 'separate spheres'.

> This paragraph provides a counter-argument to the previous paragraph, showing that the essay is balanced in its treatment of the topic.

> The sources and own knowledge are integrated throughout the paragraph, rather than the paragraph dealing with the sources then with own knowledge.

> The conclusion makes an overall judgement, referring back to the definition of 'separate spheres' set up in the introduction.

40/40

This response is strong in terms of own knowledge in analysis of the source material. In terms of the use of own knowledge, the essay receives a mark in Level 4 due to the strong focus on the question, the accuracy and detail of the supporting evidence, and due to the fact that it integrates the sources with the own knowledge to reach a fully justified conclusion. The use of the sources is also strong. The candidate selects the best evidence from the sources to support its points, and weighs this evidence to reach a conclusion.

Key terms

One of the reasons this essay is so successful is that it begins with a clear definition of the term in the question. Another example of an essay question involving a key term is below. Make a plan of your answer to this question, using the sources above. Include a definition of the key term in your introduction and refer back to this definition in subsequent paragraphs.

b) Use Sources 4, 5 and 6 and your own knowledge.

Do you agree with the view that changes to the laws relating to marriage in the period 1860–1900 challenged the idea that women should be 'the angel in the home'?

Explain your answer, using Sources 4, 5 and 6 and your own knowledge.

Section 2: Women's changing role within the political system, 1870–1920

Women and the franchise

Until 1918, all women, and many men, were excluded from voting in **national elections**. Consequently, the campaign for women's **suffrage** was part of a broader movement to extend the **franchise**.

During the nineteenth century, a series of reforms extended the franchise to a growing number of men:

Date	Act	Impact	Proportion of enfranchised men
1832	Great Reform Act	Extended the franchise to men living in industrial cities who owned property worth more than £10.	1/7
1867	Second Reform Act	Extended the franchise to 'respectable working men': men living in cities who owned property worth more than £7.	2/5
1884	Third Reform Act	Extended the franchise to agricultural labourers, all male homeowners, and all male rent-payers.	2/3

Women and local elections

Although women were excluded from national elections, some women gained the right to vote in **local elections**:

■ The Municipal Franchise Act of 1869 gave unmarried women **rate-payers** the right to vote in local council elections.

■ The 1888 County Council Act (also known as the Local Government Act) created county councils and borough councils. It entitled unmarried rate-paying women to vote in elections for these councils.

■ The 1894 Local Government Act extended local government voting rights to married women over the age of 21. It also gave women the right to stand for election to local government.

■ As a result of these Acts, by the late 1890s, 729,000 women had the right to vote in local elections in England and Wales. By 1900, women accounted for 14 per cent of the local government electorate.

Why were women excluded from national elections?

In the Victorian period, national government performed a relatively small number of tasks. It was concerned with policing, foreign policy, the **empire**, and the military. By contrast, local government had a relatively big role, dealing with education, health, welfare and housing.

The division between national and local government was related to the 'separate spheres' of men and women (see page 4). National government concerned defence and protection, and was therefore considered to be a man's domain. Local government concerned care and nurturing, which were considered appropriate to a woman's role. Therefore, it was considered legitimate for a woman to play a role in local government but not national government.

Why were married and unmarried women treated differently?

Married and unmarried women were treated differently due to the link between voting and property. Legally, votes were given to **householders** on the basis that they could vote on behalf of the whole household. In this sense, husbands represented their wives, and fathers represented their daughters. Unmarried women who set up a household alone were able to vote in local elections because they counted as householders.

The politics of 'separate spheres'

The Municipal Franchise Act of 1869 reflected a broadening of what was understood by 'separate spheres'. In the early Victorian period, it was assumed that a woman's sphere was restricted to the household. However, by 1869, women were increasingly performing caring and nurturing roles outside the household. For example, women were employed as teachers and nurses. In this sense, the role of a woman continued to be different to that of a man, but was no longer contained within the family home.

Below is a sample part (b) exam-style question which asks you how far the sources agree with a specific statement. On this page are three sources which give information relevant to the question. Identify whether the sources support, mainly support, mainly challenge, or challenge the statement in the question and then give reasons for your answer.

Use Sources 1, 2 and 3 and your own knowledge.

Do you agree with the view that the extension of the franchise to women in local elections was a significant step towards sexual equality in Britain?

SOURCE 1

(Adapted from Carol Harlow and Richard Rawlings, Pressure Through Law, *published 1992)*

One factor in the passage through Parliament of the Municipal Franchise Act of 1869 was an eight hundred strong petition. A more cynical reason is that MPs largely despised local politics and thought it a proper field of activity for women. In any event, the concession was short-lived and judges often took measures to prevent women from voting in these elections

This source <u>supports / mainly supports / mainly challenges / challenges</u> the view that the extension of the franchise to women in local elections was a significant step towards sexual equality in Britain because

_____

_____

SOURCE 2

(Adapted from The Leeds Mercury, *24 November 1869)*

A tea meeting in celebration of the local election took place last night. The fact that many ladies – their sex having this month exercised their local vote for the first time – had given their support for the two gentlemen who emerged victorious was the cause of the celebration. Mr Councillor Gaunt was glad to learn that the working men of Holbeck [a district of Leeds] had resolved to commemorate the granting of votes to women in local elections by presenting a clock to the woman who gave the first vote. He also stated that Holbeck had always been one of the first areas to embrace electoral change.

This source <u>supports / mainly supports / mainly challenges / challenges</u> the view that the extension of the franchise to women in local elections was a significant step towards sexual equality in Britain because

_____

_____

SOURCE 3

(From Frank W. Thackeray and John E. Findling, Events that Changed Great Britain since 1689, *published 2002)*

In the later decades of the nineteenth century, women gained the right to vote in local elections and to hold office at a local level. Once they received the right to vote in local elections, women frequently helped to elect women candidates to local positions. Even in local elections, women generally received support for positions that fell within 'women's' domain, such as those on boards overseeing education or poor relief. It remained difficult for women candidates to get elected to sit on town councils, mostly because the major parties did not support their nomination to these positions.

This source <u>supports / mainly supports / mainly challenges / challenges</u> the view that the extension of the franchise to women in local elections was a significant step towards sexual equality in Britain because

_____

_____

Above are a sample part (b) question and the three sources referred to in the question. In one colour, draw links between the sources to show ways in which they agree about the impact of extending the franchise to women in local elections. In another colour, draw links between the sources to show ways in which they disagree. Around the edge of the sources, write relevant own knowledge. Again, draw links to show the ways in which this agrees and disagrees with the sources.

Women, education and welfare

Revised

Education prior to 1870

Before 1870, education was provided by voluntary organisations such as charities and churches, and it was not compulsory for children to attend schools.

Changes to education happened in the early 1830s. In 1833, factories were legally required to provide part-time education for the children they employed. In 1834, the government began to provide schools for poor children by establishing **workhouse** schools.

The expansion of education

In 1870 the Elementary Education Act was introduced to provide a basic education for all children between the ages of 5 and 12. The Act provided funds to establish government-run schools in areas where there was no existing voluntary provision. The new schools were run by **School Boards**, elected by the local community.

Women and education

The expansion of education affected women in the following ways:

■ Women had the right to vote and to stand for election to the School Boards. Between 1892 and 1895, 128 women were elected to School Boards in England and Wales. Serving on the School Board was a high status role within the local community, and gave the women involved a powerful voice.

■ An increasing demand for teachers led to the expansion of teacher training colleges for women:
   – In 1879, the University of London accepted female trainee teachers.
   – In 1885, the Cambridge Training Centre for women was founded.

■ Before 1870, teaching had been a predominantly male profession. This changed following the 1870 Act, and by 1880, three-fifths of teachers were women. Indeed, by 1890, there were over twice as many female teachers as male teachers.

■ Women on School Boards and female teachers used their influence to address **gender** inequalities in schools. For example, Lydia Becker ensured that boys were taught the traditionally female skills of cooking and sewing.

Women and welfare

The Poor Law of 1834 established a system of workhouses which were intended to provide basic welfare for the poorest people. Women were involved in the administration of the workhouses in two key ways:

1 The Workhouse Visiting Society

In 1859, Louisa Twinning established the Workhouse Visiting Society, a committee of 63 highly respected people who were dedicated to improving conditions in the workhouses. Twinning also campaigned to change the public view that poor people were to blame for their own poverty.

2 Women Guardians

Each workhouse had a Guardian, a wealthy person elected from the local community. Guardians were in charge of ensuring that workhouse residents were provided for adequately. The first female Poor Law Guardian, Martha Merrington, was elected in 1875, and by 1900, there were over 1000 female Poor Law Guardians.

Education, welfare and 'separate spheres'

The participation of women in education and welfare was a broad continuation of the belief that women and men operated in 'separate spheres' (see page 4). Education and welfare were thought appropriate to a woman's natural inclination to nurture. Indeed, one of the ways in which women justified their status as Poor Law Guardians was by arguing that administering a workhouse was similar to running a family home. Nevertheless, the fact that women served alongside men on School Boards and as Poor Law Guardians blurred the distinction between the gender roles.

Below are a sample part (a) question and two paragraphs written in answer to this question. Read the question and the answers, as well as the sources. Then, using a highlighter, highlight examples of integration – where sources are used together. You cannot reach Level 3 or Level 4 of the part (a) mark scheme (see page 77) without integration of the sources. Which paragraph reaches the higher level?

Study Sources 1, 2 and 3. How far do the sources suggest that women's work as Poor Law Guardians challenged the philosophy of 'separate spheres'?

There is evidence in all three sources that women's work as Poor Law Guardians did not challenge the philosophy of 'separate spheres'. Both Sources 1 and 3 indicate that the role of a Poor Law Guardian was essentially a caring role. Source 1 argues that Poor Law Guardians were responsible for 'the care of the poor, the aged, the sick, and the miserable'. Source 3 supports this by saying that Emmeline Pankhurst, 'managed to make [the life of the poor] more endurable'. Additionally, Sources 1 and 3 use words that suggest that the work of a Guardian reflects the work that women were expected to do in the home. For example, Source 1 says that a Guardian's role relates to 'housekeeping' and 'clothing'. Similarly, Source 3 suggests that Pankhurst improved the food of the 'poorly fed' inmates. In this way, all three sources suggest that women's work as Poor Law Guardians did not challenge the philosophy of 'separate spheres' because all three Sources indicate that a woman's proper duties related to caring and the home.

Source 1 contains little evidence that women's work as Poor Law Guardians challenged the philosophy of 'separate spheres'. Rather, it stresses the fact that the work of the Poor Law Guardians was about 'housekeeping, clothing, and education' — all of which were part of a woman's domestic sphere. Source 2 suggests that women should not be appointed as Poor Law Guardians because 'their domestic responsibilities' are an embarrassment to them — meaning that women are too busy in the domestic sphere to take on the responsibility of working in a Poor House. In this sense, Source 2 presents a different argument to Source 1, as it suggests that women's domestic duties in the home are an obstacle to public service outside the home. Source 3 provides evidence of the work undertaken by Poor Law Guardians and, supporting Source 1. For example, Emmeline Pankhurst states that her role as Poor Law Guardian involved dealing with problems relating to inmates who were 'poorly fed' suggesting that her role was primarily that of a carer and therefore simply an extension of her role in the domestic sphere.

SOURCE 1

(From a campaign poster supporting the election of Louisa Edwards to the position of Poor Law Guardian in Bedford, 1887)

Women should be on a Board of Guardians because the larger number of paupers are women and children. Because the care of the poor, the aged, the sick, and the miserable is the work of Guardians. An important part of the work of Guardians is the selection of nurses and female servants. In the great matters of housekeeping, clothing, and education the staff of the workhouse rely on women Guardians.

SOURCE 2

(Adapted from The Colne and Nelson Times, *a local newspaper, March 1901. The newspaper was opposing the election of Selina Cooper as a Poor Law Guardian)*

At the risk of being described as impolite, we have to ask the electors of Nelson to see to it that the three men candidates are elected Poor Law Guardians … We hold that the interests of women are respected by committees consisting entirely of men … The three male candidates [in this election] do not have the domestic responsibilities which embarrass women.

SOURCE 3

(Adapted from Emmeline Pankhurst, My Own Story, published 1914)

A year after my return to Manchester in 1894 I became a candidate for the Board of Poor Law Guardians. I was elected, heading the poll by a large majority. When I came into office I found that the workhouse was being very harshly administered. The old board had been made up of the kind of men who like to save money. For instance, the inmates were being very poorly fed. I found the old folks in the workhouse sitting on backless benches. They had no privacy, no possessions, not even a locker. In a number of ways we managed to make their existence more endurable.

The origins of the suffrage campaign

Women and national elections

There were five main reasons why women were not allowed to vote in national elections:

- Some politicians argued that women were not interested in voting and that suffrage should only be given to groups who were interested in politics.
- Until 1869, six-sevenths of men had no right to vote. Consequently, the experience of women differed little from the experience of the majority of men.
- Politicians argued that women were represented by the votes of their husbands and fathers.
- Women were able to participate in politics without voting. Many middle-class women were involved in education or workhouse reform.
- The philosophy of 'separate spheres' (see page 4) indicated that women had no role to play in national government.

Political changes, 1870–1902

In the later Victorian period, a series of changes increased calls for women's suffrage:

- The 1867 Reform Act enfranchised the majority of working men (see page 20). From this point, the exclusion of women became more obvious.
- It became more obvious that voting conferred power on the voter. For example, following the 1867 Reform Act, pressure from working-class voters brought about rights for **trade unions**.
- As a result of the **Boer War** (1899–1902), the national government became involved in the provision of health and welfare – policy areas traditionally associated with women.

The origins of the suffrage debate

Women's suffrage was first debated in Parliament in 1867. **John Stuart Mill** proposed an amendment to the Second Reform Act which would have given women suffrage on equal terms to men. Mill's amendment was treated as a joke. Seventy-three MPs voted in favour, 196 MPs voted against, but over 400 MPs were not interested enough to vote. Mill's amendment was backed by a petition signed by 1500 men and women.

The foundation of the suffrage movement

Following the defeat of Mill's amendment, groups campaigning for women's suffrage emerged across Britain. However, there was a series of divisions which hindered the effectiveness of the movement:

The movement was split over the relationship between the campaign for suffrage and the campaign against the Contagious Diseases Acts (see page 14). Women in London believed that the two issues should be kept separate for fear that supporters of the Contagious Diseases Acts would automatically oppose female suffrage. Women outside London thought that the campaign should be united and women should fight against all discrimination.

The movement was split over the relationship between the suffrage movement and political parties. Radical women, who formed the Central National Society for Women's Suffrage (CNS), wanted to join the Liberal Party as this party was sympathetic to women's suffrage. Moderates, who formed the Central Committee for the National Society for Women's Suffrage (NSWS), believed that the suffrage movement should be independent of any political party.

The movement was split over the rights of married women. CNS argued that they should campaign for suffrage for unmarried women alone. However, the Women's Franchise League (WFrL) campaigned for equal rights for all women.

In spite of these divisions, the WFrL was successful in its campaign to extend voting rights to married women as part of the 1894 Local Government Act (see page 20).

High level answers avoid summarising or paraphrasing the sources, and instead make inferences from the sources. Below is Source 1 and a series of statements. Read the source and decide which of the statements:

- make inferences from the source (I)
- summarise the source (S)
- paraphrase the source (P)
- cannot be justified from the source (X).

Statement	I	P	S	X
Only women signed petitions in favour of women's suffrage between 1869 and 1875.				
People who supported women's suffrage worked hard to organise petitions and meetings.				
Support for women's suffrage increased in the period 1869–1875.				
Supporters of women's suffrage used legal means to campaign for the vote.				
Supporters of women's suffrage organised larger and larger petitions in favour of the vote.				

SOURCE 1

(Adapted from Sophia A. Van Wingerden, The Women's Suffrage Movement in Britain, 1866–1928, *published 1999)*

Those who were committed to women's suffrage worked hard to spread the word by means of petitions, pamphlets, and public meetings. In 1869, suffragists presented 255 petitions containing 61,475 signatures. In 1871, 622 petitions, signed by 186,976 persons. In 1872, 829 petitions, with 350,093 signatures. By 1875, the number of petitions was 1,273, with 415,622 signatures.

SOURCE 2

(Adapted from an article in The Victoria Magazine, *1869. The article describes the first parliamentary debate on women's suffrage)*

Mr Onslow [a Liberal MP] had taken some trouble to find out the opinions of ladies on the subject of women's suffrage, and a short time ago, being introduced to two ladies, he asked them what they would do with a vote if they had one. Their reply was, that they would vote for the candidate who would give them the best pair of diamond earrings. The House of Commons then divided and the motion was lost, 196 members voting against and 73 for female suffrage.

SOURCE 3

(Adapted from Constance Rover, Women's Suffrage and Party Politics in Britain, *published 1967)*

To many in Britain in the late nineteenth century, the statement that women, being women, were unfitted for the vote seemed so obvious that it needed no support. Others thought it necessary to support the statement by adding that voting was unfeminine, unnatural and that women lacked both education and political knowledge. Women's participation in local politics was approved but their direct involvement in national politics was considered undesirable.

Below is a sample part (b) exam-style question and a paragraph written in answer to this question. The question refers to the sources on this page. The paragraph contains a limited amount of own knowledge. Annotate the paragraph to add additional own knowledge to the answer.

Use Sources 1, 2 and 3 and your own knowledge.

Do you agree with the view that the main reason that women were denied the vote in the period 1869–1902 was lack of public support?

One reason why women were denied the vote in the period 1869 to 1902 was because they lacked Parliamentary support. Source 2 describes the first Parliamentary debate on women's suffrage. It notes that 'the motion was lost, 196 members voting against and 73 for women's suffrage.' In fact, most MPs did not even vote on the issue. Source 1 supports this, implying that Parliament refused to respond to an increasing number of petitions in the years 1869 to 1875. Source 3 also indicates that many felt that women lacked 'political knowledge'. Indeed, some politicians argued that women were already represented by the votes of others. This is supported by Source 2, in which a Liberal MP suggests women care more about earrings than they do about politics.

NUWSS Campaigns

The foundation of the NUWSS

The NUWSS was founded in 1897 by Millicent Fawcett. Fawcett's goal was to unite women's groups and end the splits which had undermined the movement in the 1880s. Consequently, the NUWSS began with a **decentralised** structure which allowed local groups to govern themselves and choose their own tactics. In 1907, the movement was reformed with a more centralised structure, and Fawcett became its President.

Membership of the NUWSS

The most prominent members of the NUWSS were middle-class women. However, membership also included a small number of men and – particularly in the north – working-class women. Indeed, the Lancashire and Cheshire Women Textile and Other Workers Representative Committee, founded in 1903 and affiliated to the NUWSS, focused on recruiting working-class women to the suffrage campaign.

NUWSS arguments in favour of women's suffrage

The NUWSS argued that moral character rather than gender should be the basis for suffrage. One poster argued that women could be educated, responsible parents, or the local mayor and still excluded from voting in national elections. In contrast, men could be drunkards, adulterers and uneducated and still have the vote.

Another campaign stressed women's expertise in the areas of welfare and education. One poster depicted **John Bull** looking confused at the range of issues he must now consider. Next to him stands a woman who offers to help him with these new social questions.

Campaigns

Between 1904 and 1912, the NUWSS was involved in a series of political campaigns.

Date	Campaign	Details
1904–1912	**Private Members' Bills**	The NUWSS backed individual MPs in their attempts to introduce laws to Parliament which would give women the right to vote.
1906–1912	General election and **by-election** campaigns	The NUWSS organised campaigns in parliamentary **constituencies** to persuade the major political parties to promote candidates who favoured women's suffrage. They also used the elections in order to recruit members and gain media interest in their campaign.
1910	Petition	The NUWSS organised a petition signed by 300,000 men in favour of female suffrage.

NUWSS successes

Between 1907 and 1910, NUWSS membership increased to over 50,000. In the same period, donations to the NUWSS quadrupled. However, they failed in their main objective to persuade Parliament to grant women the right to vote in national elections.

Lydia Becker

Lydia Becker was a key player in the women's suffrage movement. She was the secretary of the Manchester branch of the National Society for Women's Suffrage, founded in 1867. In addition, she founded the *Women's Suffrage Journal*.

Becker was the key strategist for the women's movement and her death in 1890 was a turning point in the campaign for women's suffrage. Following her death, there was an attempt to reorganise the movement with the creation of the National Union of Women's Suffrage Societies (NUWSS).

Millicent Fawcett

During the 1870s, Millicent Fawcett became a well-known public speaker, and was involved in the campaign against the Contagious Diseases Acts. During the 1880s, she acted as a **conciliator** between the different factions of the women's movement. In 1871 she co-founded Newnham College in Cambridge (see page 56). Fawcett was married to a prominent Liberal MP and was committed to working with the political establishment in her campaign for women's suffrage.

Doing reliability well

Below are a series of definitions listing common reasons why sources are reliable or unreliable, and Sources 1 and 2. Under each source, explain why the source is either reliable or unreliable for the purpose stated, justifying your answer by referring to the following definitions.

- **Vested interest:** the source is written so that the writer can protect their power or their financial interests.
- **Second-hand report:** the writer of the source is not an eyewitness, but is relying on someone else's account.
- **Expertise:** the source is written on a subject which the author (for example a historian) is an expert.
- **Political bias:** a source is written by someone with strong political views and reflects these views.
- **Reputation:** a source is written to protect the writer's reputation.

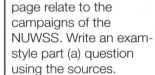

Write the question

The sources on this page relate to the campaigns of the NUWSS. Write an exam-style part (a) question using the sources.

Study Sources 1, 2 and 3.

How far do the sources agree that

_____
_____
_____
_____
_____
_____
_____
_____
_____
_____

SOURCE 1

(Adapted from Elizabeth Robins, Way Station, *1913. Elizabeth Robins was a suffragist. Here, she describes a joint NUWSS and WSPU march that was held in 1908)*

On June 21st an impressive historical and symbolic pageant, organised by the NUWSS, marched through crowded, cheering streets. Under the chairmanship of Mrs Fawcett a mass meeting was held of such size and enthusiasm that men of long political experience declared it had seldom been equalled.

The source is reliable / fairly reliable / fairly unreliable / unreliable *as evidence of public support for the suffrage movement in 1908 because*

_____

_____

SOURCE 3

(Adapted from a report of the Annual Council of the NUWSS, 25 October 1907)

The main idea underlying the by-election scheme is the education of constituencies in women's suffrage, and the use of these elections as an opportunity for organising new women's suffrage societies. A by-election offers the best opportunity for getting the attention of voters.

SOURCE 2

(From a pamphlet published by the NUWSS in 1911)

The NUWSS has grown into a large and powerful body, its progress during the last two years being especially remarkable. In January 1909, there were 70 affiliated societies. In January 1911, there were 204 affiliated societies. Societies of the NUWSS are now, therefore, in existence in all parts of Great Britain. Some of them work in a considerable number of Parliamentary constituencies.

The source is reliable / fairly reliable / fairly unreliable / unreliable *as evidence of public support for the suffrage movement in 1908 because*

_____

_____

WSPU campaigns: deeds not words

The Women's Social and Political Union (WSPU) was founded by **Emmeline Pankhurst** in 1903. It believed that a more radical campaign would force the government to give women the vote.

The structure of the WSPU

The WSPU was accused of being more centralised and **autocratic** than the NUWSS. Most of the leaders of the WSPU were the friends and family of Emmeline Pankhurst. Indeed, Pankhurst's daughters, Christabel, Sylvia and Adela played key roles in the campaign. Opponents accused Pankhurst of hypocrisy as she used an undemocratic organisation to campaign for democracy. Pankhurst argued that strong leadership was needed in order to achieve decisive action. The WSPU newspaper, *Votes for Women*, was founded by **Frederick and Emmeline Pethick-Lawrence**, who also provided substantial financial support for the organisation.

Suffragettes and suffragists

The NUWSS described themselves as suffragists as they were campaigning for women's suffrage. The WSPU were nicknamed 'suffragettes' by the *Daily Mail* in 1906. 'Suffragette' was a play on the word 'suffragist', with the ending 'ette' meaning small and feminine.

Early suffragette campaigns

Whereas the NUWSS lobbied politicians and presented petitions to Parliament, the suffragettes preferred **direct action**.

Date	Protest
1905	Annie Kenney and Christabel Pankhurst **heckled** the MP **Winston Churchill** during a speech in Manchester. Subsequently, suffragettes heckled MPs speaking in Parliament.
1908	Suffragettes threw stones at windows in a building where Churchill was speaking.
1908	Suffragettes organised a **'Trojan horse'** raid on Parliament. Twenty-six suffragettes leapt out of a van outside the House of Commons and tried to force their way in.

Increasing militancy

From 1908, the protests of the suffragettes became increasingly **militant**. Radical suffragettes argued that outrageous tactics were necessary in order to get media attention.

Date	Protest
1908	Flora Drummond chained herself to the railings outside Number 10 Downing Street.
1909	The suffragettes declared their support for the Tax Resistance League, an organisation that encouraged women to refuse to pay tax until they got the vote.
1911	The suffragettes organised a campaign of census evasion, urging women to withhold details from the government.
1911	**Emily Davison** set fire to a post-box.
1912	The suffragettes organised a window smashing campaign.
1913	The suffragettes organised an **arson** attack on the home of **David Lloyd George**.
1913	Emily Davison threw herself underneath the King's horse during the Epsom Derby. She died from her injuries.
1914	A suffragette attacked with an axe **Velazquez's painting of Venus** at the National Gallery.

Hunger strikes and force-feeding

Suffragettes who were imprisoned for their illegal protests rebelled by going on **hunger strike**. Initially, the authorities responded by force-feeding the hunger-strikers. The force-feeding provoked outrage amongst the public. Consequently, in 1913, the Liberal government passed the **'Cat and Mouse Act'** allowing hunger-strikers to be released from prison.

Successes of the suffragettes

The suffragettes succeeded in keeping media attention focused on the issue of women's votes. The media were fascinated by the suffragettes' tactic of dressing in a feminine fashion whilst committing acts that were seen as unladylike. However, much of the publicity was critical, drawing links between the suffragettes' actions and the stereotype of women as hysterical. Consequently, the NUWSS accused the suffragettes of alienating public support for women's suffrage.

Use the information on the opposite page to add detail to the Venn diagram below. On either side of the diagram list aims and methods unique to the NUWSS and the WSPU. In the centre, list aims and methods that the two organisations shared.

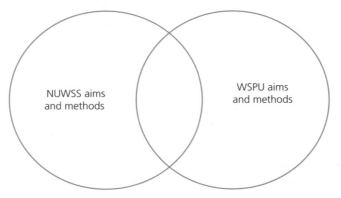

NUWSS aims and methods

WSPU aims and methods

Linking sources

Below is a sample part (a) question and on this page are the three sources referred to in the question. In one colour, draw links between the sources to show ways in which they agree about the treatment of the attitude of the army leaders. In another colour, draw links between the sources to show ways in which they disagree.

Study Sources 1, 2 and 3.

How far do the sources suggest that the militant campaigns of the suffragettes succeeded in attracting public sympathy?

SOURCE 1

(Adapted from The Morning Post, *June 1914. The newspaper is describing the trial of men accused of attacking suffragettes)*

Police-constable Paul described the efforts of the young men to throw the militant suffragettes into a pond. The judge said he would not impose any penalty on this occasion. He said it was impossible to shut one's eyes to the fact that the behaviour of these women had created strong resentment and disgust.

SOURCE 3

(Adapted from The Star, *31 October 1906)*

There is not the slightest doubt that the suffragettes are political prisoners, and ought not to be treated as common criminals. The Jameson Raiders* were guilty of a more serious crime, yet they were not denied the privileges of receiving letters. They were not asked to sleep on the plank bed and to live on a meagre prison diet. However, from the point of view of agitation in favour of Women's Suffrage, the more martyrs that are made the better for the cause.

*The Jameson Raid was an attempt to overthrow the Dutch government in South Africa. The Raiders were arrested and imprisoned in Britain.

SOURCE 2

(From Daily Mirror, *29 April 1906)*

The impact of the First World War on the suffrage campaign

The First World War had an immediate impact on the campaign for women's suffrage and was one factor which contributed to the enfranchisement of women.

Suffragist and suffragette actions during the war

On the outbreak of war in August 1914, the NUWSS and the WSPU ceased their public campaigns, agreeing that women had a patriotic duty to support the war effort. Consequently, the suffragettes and the suffragists encouraged women to take over the jobs of men who were fighting. At the same time, they continued to lobby government ministers to grant women the vote. During the war, the WSPU and the NUWSS continued to campaign for the rights of women in the following ways:

	WSPU actions	NUWSS actions
Work	In collaboration with Lloyd George, Emmeline Pankhurst organised the Women's Right to Serve demonstration in July 1917. The march was intended to encourage women to take jobs in industry. The government provided £2000 to support the march. Emmeline Pankhurst suggested the creation of the **Women's Land Army**. In addition, Emmeline Pankhurst used her influence with trade unions to persuade them not to strike over pay and conditions.	The NUWSS set up an employment register recording women's skills so that as soon as a vacancy came up they could recommend a woman to fill it.
Health		The NUWSS supported local government initiatives to set up maternity centres, providing healthcare and advice to pregnant women and new mothers. Fawcett argued that protecting young lives was of particular importance during wartime.
Lobbying	Emmeline Pankhurst put pressure on Lloyd George to support women's suffrage.	In March 1917, Millicent Fawcett arranged to meet Lloyd George to request that women be given the vote once the war had ended. Emmeline Pankhurst was later invited to this meeting.

Divisions in the movement

In spite of efforts by leading members of the WSPU and the NUWSS to support the war effort, some campaigners opposed the war, leading to splits in both the NUWSS and the WSPU.

The East London Federation of Suffragettes

Sylvia Pankhurst was bitterly opposed to the war. Therefore, she withdrew from the WSPU and started the East London Federation of Suffragettes (ELFS). She became so radical that she publically praised the **Bolshevik Revolution** in Russia, arguing that sexual equality would only be possible in Britain following a **Communist** revolution. The ELFS also campaigned for better pay for women during the war and opposed Regulation 40D which criminalised sex between women with sexually transmitted diseases and members of the armed forces.

The Women's International League for Peace and Freedom

In 1915, tensions within the NUWSS led to the establishment of the Women's International League for Peace and Freedom. Some radical members of the NUWSS, such as Isabella Ford and Helena Swanwick, believed that war was the inevitable outcome of male aggression.

> **The impact of the suffrage movement on women's suffrage**
>
> Despite divisions during wartime, the suffrage movement played a major role in gaining women the vote in 1918. Together, the NUWSS and the WSPU kept the issue of women's voting rights at the top of the political agenda through ceaseless lobbying and headline-grabbing direct action. The patriotism shown by both groups during the war also helped to persuade male politicians that the time had come to give women the vote.

Spectrum of significance

Below is a sample part (b) exam-question and a list of general points which could be used to answer the question. Use your own knowledge and the information on the opposite page to reach a judgement about the importance of these general points to the question posed. Write numbers on the spectrum below to indicate their relative importance. Having done this, write a brief justification of your placement, explaining why some of these factors are more important than others. The resulting diagram could form the basis of an essay plan.

Do you agree with the view that women's work during the First World War was the most significant reason for the granting of female suffrage in 1918?

1. NUWSS campaigns before the First World War.
2. WSPU campaigns before the First World War.
3. Women's work in the First World War.
4. NUWSS and WSPU actions during the First World War.

← —————————————————————————— →

Very important   Less important

Recommended reading

Below is a list of suggested further reading on this topic.

- Paula Bartley, *Votes for Women 1860–1928*, pages 48–61, (2007)
- Harold L. Smith, *British Feminism in the Early Twentieth Century,* pages 7–22, (1990)
- Susan Kingsley Kent, *Sex and Suffrage in Britain 1860–1914*, pages 197–205, (1990)

Exam focus

On pages 33–35 are sample answers to the exam-style questions on this page. Read the answers and the examiner comments around them.

(a) Study Sources 1, 2 and 3.

How far do the Sources suggest that the WSPU's militant campaigns diminished public support for the suffrage movement?

Explain your answer, using the evidence of Sources 1, 2 and 3. **(20 marks)**

(b) Use Sources 4, 5 and 6 and your own knowledge.

Do you agree with the view that the women's role in local government simply 'confirmed their domestic role' in the years 1860–1914?

Explain your answer, using Sources 4, 5 and 6 and your own knowledge. **(40 marks)**

SOURCE 1

(Adapted from Emmeline Pankhurst, My Own Story, *published 1914. In 1911 Pankhurst was arrested and charged with encouraging other women to damage property. She describes the reaction of the jury at the end of the trial)*

The jury was absent for more than an hour, showing that they had some difficulty in agreeing upon a verdict. The foreman's* voice shook as he pronounced the guilty verdict. He had hard work to control his emotion as he spoke to the judge: 'Your Lordship, we hope that you will consider the pure motives that have led to this trouble, and that you will not be harsh when you deal with this case.' A burst of applause followed his speech.

*The foreman is the chair of the jury and speaks on behalf of the jury at the end of a trial.

SOURCE 2

(From a report in the Daily Telegraph *from 11 March 1912)*

Thirty-two women were sentenced to imprisonment with hard labour at Bow-Street on Saturday for window breaking. Appeals were made to the magistrate on the ground that the defendants were carried away by the example of hysterical women.

Two suffragists tried to address a meeting outside the court but were not allowed to speak. The crowd jeered and threw eggs, oranges, banana skins, and a bag of flour.

SOURCE 3

(Adapted from Millicent Fawcett's letter to The Times *of 8 June 1914)*

The National Union of Women's Suffrage Societies and all other law-abiding suffragists – the vast majority of the whole movement – are deeply distressed by the continuance of violent crime by a small group of fanatics. We have again and again expressed our detestation of crime. But punishment will never solve the problem of political militancy. The surest way to prevent violence is political reform.

SOURCE 4

(Adapted from Sandra Burman, Fit Work for Women, *published 1979)*

[From 1850] women were appointed to public positions. Unpaid women bore much of the cost of government welfare before the First World War. They assisted as inspectors of midwives and became involved in education provision. Women were recruited as local government workers, but in a way that confirmed their domestic role and their financial dependence upon men.

SOURCE 5

(Adapted from Norman McCord, Bill Purdue, A. William Purdue, British History 1815–1914, *published 2007)*

From 1896 unmarried female ratepayers could vote in borough elections. By 1900 about a million women in England and Wales possessed a local franchise. This advance was not universally welcomed. The Local Government Act of 1888 excluded women from standing for election in the new County Councils.

SOURCE 6

(Adapted from Millicent Fawcett, Women's Suffrage: A Short History of A Great Movement, *published 1912)*

At the first School Board election which took place in London in November 1870, Miss Elizabeth Garrett MD and Miss Emily Davies were elected as members. Miss Garrett won the most votes in her constituency of Marylebone. In Edinburgh Miss Flora Stevenson was elected to the first School Board. From the date of her election she was appointed by her colleagues to act as convener of the most important committees, and in 1900 was unanimously elected the chairman of the School Board.

(a) Study Sources 1, 2 and 3.

How far do the Sources suggest that the WSPU's militant campaigns diminished public support for the suffrage movement?

Explain your answer, using the evidence of Sources 1, 2 and 3. **(20 marks)**

Overall, Sources 1, 2 and 3 indicate that the WSPU's militant campaign did diminish public support for the suffrage movement. However, they do not indicate that public support was entirely lost. Rather, they indicate that some sections of the public objected to militant methods without rejecting the goals of the suffrage campaign.

> The first sentence clearly answers the question.

Source 2 suggests strongly that WSPU militancy diminished public support for the suffrage movement. It reports that following militant action 'Two suffragists tried to address a meeting ... but were not allowed to speak.' This shows that WSPU violence affected the whole movement, as public sympathy for the suffragists, a different wing of the suffrage movement, also decreased. Source 1 provides some evidence to support this as the foreman of the jury assumes that the judge will be 'harsh' with Emmeline Pankhurst after she was charged with encouraging women to destroy property. Source 3 also indicates that WSPU violence was a problem for the movement as Millicent Fawcett is forced to defend the movement in her letter to The Times by arguing that the NUWSS was 'deeply distressed by the continuing violent crime' of the WSPU. Clearly, all three sources agree that suffragette violence had a negative impact on public support for the movement, as shown by the reaction of the public in Source 2, the foreman's comments in Source 1, and Fawcett's defence of the movement in Source 3.

> By considering evidence that militancy diminished public support for the suffrage movement first, the essay is directly focusing on the question.

> This paragraph clearly links the account given in Source 2 with the account given in Source 3, therefore comparing the sources in detail.

However, there is also evidence in all three sources to suggest that WSPU violence did not cause everyone to lose sympathy for the suffrage movement. Source 1 indicates that the jury dealing with Emmeline Pankhurst was sympathetic to her cause. The source notes that the jury were 'absent for more than an hour, showing that they had some difficulty in agreeing upon a verdict.' The jury also asked the judge to be lenient. Finally, there was support for the jury's request in the courtroom as the foreman's speech was followed by 'a burst of applause.' Therefore, Source 1 indicates that the jury condemned the violence, but had sympathy towards the cause. This is exactly the message given in Source 3 in which Fawcett condemns 'violent crime by a small group of fanatics,' but calls for 'political reform' — that is to say, the granting of women's suffrage, in response to this. The fact that Source 1 and Source 3 agree is significant as they are written by Pankhurst and Fawcett who had different views on the militant campaigns of the WSPU, Pankhurst clearly supporting them, and Fawcett rejecting them. This unexpected agreement about the reaction of the public to WSPU campaigns indicates that militancy did not erode public support for women's suffrage. Source 2 goes even further, indicating that 'Thirty-two women' copied the example of the militant campaigners, suggesting that they found militant action an attractive means of campaigning for the vote.

> Here, the candidate refers to the different opinions of Fawcett and Pankhurst demonstrating a sophisticated understanding of the historical context of the sources.

Overall, all three sources indicate that WSPU violence had some impact on public support for the suffrage movement, but that many people remained convinced that the suffrage campaigners should be treated sympathetically.

> The conclusion is a brief summary of both sides of the argument. A more developed conclusion would be needed for full marks.

18/20

The essay on page 33 gets a mark in Level 4 because it selects relevant information from the sources, it contains a detailed comparison of the similarities and differences in the sources, and uses the provenance of the sources to consider how far WSPU militancy undermined public support for the suffrage movement.

(b) Use Sources 4, 5 and 6 and your own knowledge.

Do you agree with the view that the women's role in local government simply 'confirmed their domestic role' in the years 1860–1914?

Explain your answer, using Sources 4, 5 and 6 and your own knowledge.
(40 marks)

Source 4 clearly argues that women's role in local government largely confirmed their domestic role in the period 1860–1914. This is because women were involved in local government in ways which emphasised their role as caregivers. However, the other sources provide evidence that the women's involvement in local government was more complicated than Source 4 suggests.

Source 4 is clear that women's work in local government 'confirmed their domestic role'. Source 4 points to the fact that women were employed 'as inspectors of midwives'. This indicates that women were employed in caring roles which mirrored their domestic responsibilities. Indeed, from 1859 women worked with the Workhouse Visiting Society, and from 1875, following the election of Martha Merrington as the first female Poor Law Guardian, women were involved in local government looking after the poor. In both roles, women were operating in the domestic sphere. Furthermore, women's involvement as voters in local government, noted in Source 5, was often justified by contrasting the role of local government, which dealt with essentially domestic concerns such as education, health and welfare, with national government, which dealt with more 'masculine' policies such as policing, the military and the empire. This allowed women to argue for greater enfranchisement in local elections, and as Source 5 notes, 'by 1900 about a million women in England and Wales possessed a local franchise.' Source 6 describes women's role in local education, stating that 'Elizabeth Garrett ... and Emily Davies were elected as members' of the first School Boards. Nonetheless, women's involvement in public educational administration dated back to 1834, when education was provided by workhouses, and again emphasised their caring role. Finally, Source 4 argues that the fact that women performed unpaid work for local government stressed their 'financial dependence upon men' and therefore highlighted their traditional role. In this way, women's role in local government confirmed their domestic role because local government concerned caring for people in a way similar to that expected of a wife and a mother.

In Source 6, Millicent Fawcett, leader of the NUWSS, clearly argues that women's involvement in local government was a major step forward for women. She argues that women were elected and re-elected to important positions in local school boards. Indeed, between 1892 and 1895, 128 women were elected to school boards in England and Wales. Moreover, Fawcett notes that Flora Stephenson

The introduction shows that the essay will consider both sides of the argument, and will reach an overall judgement.

This paragraph begins with a clear focus on the question.

Here, the candidate integrates the sources with own knowledge to make a clear point about the domestic role of women in local government.

Having considered evidence from all three sources and own knowledge, the paragraph ends with a statement summarising the argument of the paragraph.

'was appointed by her colleagues to act as convenor of the most important committees and was ... elected chairman of the School Board.' We can infer from Fawcett's comments that the other members of the school boards were men. This shows that women were appointed to positions where they were given authority over men, in contrast to their domestic role where they were expected to be subservient to their fathers and husbands. Indeed, women on school boards, such as Lydia Becker, used their influence to promote equality between boys and girls within schools. For example, Becker ensured that boys were taught to cook and sew. Clearly, women's involvement in the provision of education allowed them to challenge traditional gender roles by taking on high-status jobs in the local community, giving them equal, or sometimes superior, status to men.

Additionally, Source 6 suggests that the government of education was dominated by men, and therefore not exclusively linked to the domestic sphere. Evidence that suggests that local government was considered beyond a woman's role comes from Source 5, which notes that the Local Government Act of 1888 excluded women from standing for election. Together, these points indicate that there was no consensus on the link between involvement in local government and the domestic sphere, suggesting that women's involvement in local government did not simply confirm their domestic role. Equally, following the Boer War, national government was becoming increasingly concerned with the provision of welfare, and yet women were not granted the vote in national elections until 1918. This suggests that in the period 1860–1914, the link between the domestic sphere and local government was blurring.

In conclusion, although Source 4 makes a strong case that women's involvement in local government simply confirmed their domestic role, Sources 5 and 6 indicate that the picture was more complex. Source 5 describes women's exclusion from local government, while Source 6 points to the fact that women were allowed to exercise authority over men. Therefore, neither source draws a clear link between local government and women's domestic role. Also, national government, particularly under the Liberals, was becoming more involved in welfare, and in this sense too, blurred the distinction further. Overall, women's involvement in local government gave them status in the community, and real power over important issues, and therefore did not simply confirm their domestic role.

The candidate does not just take the sources at face value, but makes an inference from the evidence in Source 6, showing confident handling of the source material and allowing a more sophisticated argument.

This paragraph is weaker in terms of own knowledge. The essay would benefit from an example of national government involvement in welfare provision, such as the Provision of Meals Act (see page 52).

The conclusion supports the argument presented in the introduction, and developed throughout the essay, showing a consistent approach to the question.

36/40

This essay is very strong but does not get full marks due to the fairly limited extent of the own knowledge used. The own knowledge is accurate, focused, relevant and integrated with the sources, but a greater range and depth of own knowledge would be necessary to get full marks. The sources are used comprehensively to develop points of support and challenge and their evidence is weighed in the conclusion to reach an overall judgement.

Reverse engineering

The best essays are based on careful plans. Read both essays and the examiner's comments and try to work out the general points of the plans used to write the essays.

Section 3: Attitudes of politicians, parliament and the public to the suffrage question

Political parties and the suffrage question

All of the major political parties were split on the issue of women's suffrage.

Party	Supporters of women's suffrage	Opponents of women's suffrage
Liberal Party	Many **Liberals** believed that men and women should have equal political rights. From 1867 to 1886, the Liberals were responsible for two-thirds of the votes cast in favour of women's **suffrage** in the House of Commons. Leading figures in the Party, such as **David Lloyd George** and **Winston Churchill**, supported women's suffrage in principle. However, for reasons of political advantage, they were unwilling to back **bills** which gave voting rights to wealthy women.	**William Gladstone** believed that women were too feminine to be involved in politics. **Henry Campbell Bannerman** supported women's suffrage in private, but did not feel that it was a priority to change the law. **Herbert Asquith** believed that women could exert political influence through their husbands and fathers.
Conservative Party	For reasons of electoral advantage, most Conservative Party leaders were sympathetic towards enfranchising wealthy women. Just under half of the **private member's bills** relating to female suffrage in the period 1874–1903 were put forward by Conservatives. Sir **Arthur Balfour**, Conservative Prime Minister from 1902 until 1905, was sympathetic to women's suffrage but did not believe that his Party would back a change in the law.	**Lord Curzon**, and many in the Party, argued that women were too emotionally unstable to use the vote responsibly.
Labour Party	The Labour Party was in favour of **universal suffrage**. In 1912, the Labour Party became the first major party to officially endorse suffrage for women.	The Labour Party would not support bills that extended voting rights to wealthy women alone. Additionally, some Labour MPs, such as **Ramsey MacDonald**, believed that the struggle for women's suffrage was a distraction from the struggle for the rights of working people.

Women's suffrage and electoral advantage

Electoral advantage was often more important than principles in explaining politicians' views about women's suffrage. Changing the make-up of the electorate would impact the fortunes of the major parties. Generally, richer voters favoured the Conservative Party, whereas poorer voters favoured the Liberals or Labour. For this reason, the Liberals refused to back changes which would enfranchise property-owning (and therefore, wealthy) women. Equally, the Conservative Party did not want to enfranchise all women, as it was assumed that the majority would support the Liberals and Labour.

Electoral advantage became especially significant following the 1910 General Election. This resulted in a **hung Parliament** with 272 Liberal MPs and 272 Conservative MPs. The balance of power was so fragile that any change in the electoral register would be significant.

Political organisations

All three Parties recognised that women had influence over the way that men voted. For this reason, they established organisations designed to increase women's involvement in politics. The Conservatives founded the Primrose League in 1883, the Liberal Party created the Women's Liberal Federation in 1886, and the Labour Party set up the Women's Labour League in 1906.

Mind map

Use the information on the opposite page to add detail to the mind map below.

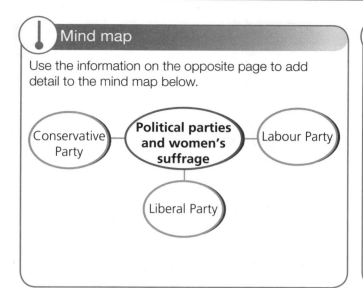

Support or challenge?

Below is a sample part (a) exam-style question which asks you how far the sources agree with a specific statement. Below this are three sources which give information relevant to the question. Identify whether the sources support, mainly support, mainly challenge, or challenge the statement in the question and then give reasons for your answer.

Study Sources 1, 2 and 3.

How far do the sources suggest that the Conservative Party broadly favoured the extension of suffrage to women in the period 1886–1914?

SOURCE 1

(Adapted from The Adelaide Advertiser, 21 May 1909)

Vigorous speeches were made by Lord Curzon at a meeting of the Men's League held last night for the purpose of opposing women's suffrage. Lord Curzon said the bulk of married women were not in favour of the suffrage. The wives of the workers were either indifferent or hostile to it. It would be impossible to enfranchise women who owned property and refuse the vote to others.

This source <u>supports / mainly supports / mainly challenges / challenges</u> the view that the Conservative Party broadly favoured the extension of suffrage to women in the period 1886–1914 because

_____

_____

SOURCE 2

(From a resolution passed at the Conservative Party Conference in 1887)

In the opinion of this conference the time has now arrived when the Parliamentary franchise may with perfect safety be extended to women householders.

This source <u>supports / mainly supports / mainly challenges</u> / challenges the view that the Conservative Party broadly favoured the extension of suffrage to women in the period 1886–1914 because

_____

_____

SOURCE 3

(From a letter to the editor of The Times, 24 November 1908. The author was a supporter of the Conservative Party)

I am writing now because I see to my great regret that the Conservative women have started a suffrage league. Women, like myself, who oppose this have formed an anti-suffrage league, conducted, as I feel sure the Conservative suffrage league will be also, peacefully.

This source <u>supports / mainly supports / mainly challenges / challenges</u> the view that the Conservative Party broadly favoured the extension of suffrage to women in the period 1886–1914 because

_____

_____

Asquith and the Conciliation Bills

The 1906 General Election ended ten years of Conservative government. Suffrage campaigners assumed that the new Liberal government would introduce a suffrage act. However, Herbert Asquith, Liberal Prime Minister from 1908, was totally opposed to women's suffrage.

The Conciliation Bills, 1910–1912

The Conciliation Committee

The Conciliation Committee was established in 1910 to gain cross-party support for a law to enfranchise some women. It was created by Lord Lytton, a Conservative Lord, and comprised a group of MPs representing all parties: 25 Liberals, 17 Conservatives, and 6 Labour MPs. The Committee supported a private member's bill which proposed to give the vote to all women householders.

> **Making a Law**
>
> In order for a bill to become a law, it must go through several stages. These include the First Reading, the Second Reading, the Committee Stage, the Third Reading, and then it has to be passed by the **House of Lords**. The Bill can be defeated at any one of these stages.
>
> Parliament works to a timetable and allocates a set amount of time to each bill. If the bill is not passed within that time, it fails.

The First Conciliation Bill, 1910

The First Conciliation Bill won a majority of Parliamentary approval in June 1910. However, Parliament was **dissolved** before the Bill could become law. As a result, the Conciliation Committee was forced to reintroduce the Bill after the 1910 General Election.

> **Black Friday, 18 November 1910**
>
> The WSPU marked the failure of the Bill with Black Friday. Many of the women who took part in the three-hundred-strong protest were assaulted by police. Pictures of suffragettes being manhandled by police in Parliament Square were a public relations disaster for Asquith's government.

The Second Conciliation Bill, 1911

In May 1911, the Second Conciliation Bill, identical in content to the First Bill, received overwhelming support in the House of Commons. However, Parliamentary debates about the Bill were so protracted that it was not passed before it ran out of time. Therefore, the Bill failed to become law. Nonetheless, Lloyd George, at the time Chancellor of the Exchequer, promised that the government would allocate the Third Conciliation Bill more Parliamentary time.

The Third Conciliation Bill and the Franchise Bill, 1912

Two bills were introduced in 1912 which had the potential to grant women suffrage: the Third Conciliation Bill and the Franchise Bill. The Third Conciliation Bill, identical to the previous Conciliation Bills, gained a majority of Parliamentary support in February 1912.

The Franchise Bill was designed to extend the franchise to men who were not householders. Asquith argued that the Bill could be amended to give women the vote. Asquith was not in favour of enfranchising women. Indeed, he assumed that the amendment would be rejected. Rather, he wanted to distract attention from the Third Conciliation Bill, ensuring its failure. In this sense, the Franchise Bill was an attempt to undermine the work of the Conciliation Committee.

Asquith's tactics paid off. The **Speaker of the House of Commons** argued that the **amendment** fundamentally changed the meaning of the Franchise Bill. Therefore, he ruled the Bill out of order and the Bill failed. At the same time, the Third Conciliation Bill ran out of time and failed to become a law.

Spot the mistake

Below are a sample exam-style part(b) question, one of the sources referred to in the question, and a paragraph written in answer to the question. Why does this paragraph not get into Level 4 for AO1? Once you have identified the mistake, rewrite the paragraph so that it displays the qualities of Level 4. The mark scheme on page 78 will help you.

Use Sources 1, 2 and 3 and your own knowledge.

Do you agree with the view that in the years 1886–1914, the Liberal Party supported women's suffrage?

> Source 1 shows that some Liberal MPs did support women's suffrage. For example, it mentions both Lloyd George and Churchill, stating that they both 'advocated women's suffrage at various meetings.' The Source also indicates that they did not support the first two Conciliation Bills, but it suggests they opposed the Bills because they would have given the electoral advantage to the Conservatives, rather than because they opposed women's suffrage. Indeed, the Source suggests that both Lloyd George and Churchill were willing to play political games to ensure the Bills were not passed, such as starting 'a rumour that Herbert Asquith would resign if the Bill was passed.' The Conciliation Bills were proposed in 1910, 1911 and 1912 during a Liberal Government. They were drawn up by the Conciliation Committee, which included 25 Liberal MPs, and proposed giving the vote to all women householders. Prior to these Bills, Liberal MPs had supported measures in favour of women's suffrage. Indeed, prior to 1886, Liberal MPs had cast two-thirds of the votes in Parliament in favour of women's suffrage Bills.

SOURCE 1

(*From Paula Bartley*, Votes for Women 1860–1928, *third edition, published 2007*)

Women's suffrage drew support from leading Liberal MPs, but this support was sometimes fainthearted. Both Lloyd George and Churchill advocated women's suffrage at various meetings, but opposed the First Conciliation Bill of 1910 because it offered too limited a female franchise that might favour the Conservatives. In 1912, when a further Conciliation Bill was being debated in Parliament, both Lloyd George and Churchill were associated with a rumour that Herbert Asquith would resign if the Bill were passed.

Spot the inference

High level answers avoid summarising or paraphrasing the sources, and instead make inferences from the sources. Below is a series of statements. Read Source 1 above and decide which of the statements:

- make inferences from the source (I)
- paraphrase the source (P)
- summarise the source (S)
- cannot be justified from the source (X).

Statement	I	P	S	X
To Lloyd George and Churchill, electoral advantage was more important than the principle that women should be allowed to vote.				
Most Liberals supported women's suffrage.				
Asquith opposed the Second Conciliation Bill.				
Lloyd George and Churchill promoted women's suffrage at meetings, but did not support the First Conciliation Bill.				
Lloyd George and Churchill supported women's suffrage, but not the Conciliation Bills.				

The NUWSS and the Labour Party

Revised

The impact of the Conciliation Bills

Although they had no formal link to the Liberal Party, many leading members of the NUWSS were also members of the Women's Liberal Federation, and had believed that the Liberal Government would support a bill to enfranchise women. Following the repeated defeat of the Conciliation Bills, the leadership of the NUWSS became disillusioned with the Liberal Party.

The failure of the Conciliation Bills led many NUWSS members to resign from the Women's Liberal Federation. Additionally, Millicent Fawcett began to consider a closer relationship with the Labour Party. Labour was an attractive alternative because:

- Since 1910, all Labour MPs had voted for every suffrage bill presented to Parliament.
- In 1912, the Labour Party Conference officially committed the Party to supporting women's suffrage.
- There were already informal alliances between the regional branches of the Labour Party and organisations affiliated to the NUWSS.
- The Liberal government was a **minority government** and consequently relied on the Labour Party for support. This meant that the Labour Party, although small, had considerable influence in Parliament.

The Election Fighting Fund (EFF)

In April 1912, leaders of the NUWSS met with leaders of the Labour Party and agreed to set up the Election Fighting Fund (EFF). The EFF was designed to raise money to support Labour candidates fighting **by-elections**. To this end, it aimed to raise £10,000.

The EFF was very effective. During 1912, there were four by-elections. The EFF provided funds for all of the Labour candidates. Three of the candidates were successful. Subsequently, the EFF began to raise money for the next General Election. By the end of 1913, they had raised £45,000.

The EFF and the NUWSS

The pact with Labour was controversial within the NUWSS. Many felt that the NUWSS should retain its political independence.

Fawcett justified the creation of the EFF by arguing that NUWSS support for Labour would put pressure on the Liberals to take women's suffrage seriously. Fawcett believed that the only way to achieve women's suffrage was through a government-backed bill. In this way, the creation of the EFF was less an endorsement of Labour, and more a strategic move designed to force the Liberal Government to throw its weight behind a suffrage bill.

To ensure that the NUWSS remained politically independent, the EFF agreed not to fund Labour candidates who stood against Liberals with a proven track record of supporting women's rights.

Friends of Women's Suffrage

The arrangement with Labour heightened the NUWSS's focus on working-class women. Soon after the EFF was founded, suffragist activists set up the Friends of Women's Suffrage scheme which was designed to recruit suffragists from the working class.

George Lansbury

George Lansbury was the most outspoken advocate of women's rights amongst Labour MPs. He proposed that Labour MPs should vote against all Liberal government measures until the government passed female suffrage legislation. However, Labour leaders rejected his proposals as too antagonistic.

George Lansbury was so determined to advance the cause of women's suffrage that he resigned his seat and fought a by-election, backed by the EFF, to highlight the issue of women's suffrage. He was not successful.

Explain the difference

Sources 1 and 2 give different accounts of the effectiveness of the alliance between the NUWSS and the Labour Party. List the ways in which the sources differ. Explain the differences between the sources using the provenance of the sources alone. The provenance appears at the top of the source in brackets.

SOURCE 1

(Adapted from an Election Fighting Fund pamphlet, 1914)

The Liberal Party and the Conservative Party are today threatened by Labour, and the central fact is that workers will increasingly be associated with the political aims of women. The suffragists are in every direction reinforcing Labour and influencing the vote on which depends the fates of Governments.

SOURCE 2

(Adapted from the minutes of the Executive Committee of the Election Fighting Fund, 6 December 1912)

Miss Courtney reported that she and Miss Marshall had interviewed Mr Mallon, the author of the very damaging article in the *Labour Leader** and had made him understand the real situation with regard to women's suffrage.

*The *Labour Leader* was a publication produced by the Labour Party.

 Eliminate irrelevance

Below is a sample part (a) exam-style question that refers to Sources 1 and 2 above and Source 3 below. There is also a paragraph written in answer to this question. Read the paragraph and identify parts of the paragraph that are not directly relevant to the question. Draw a line through the information that is irrelevant and justify your deletions in the margin.

Study sources 1, 2 and 3.

How far do the sources agree on the effectiveness of the pact between the NUWSS and the Labour Party?

There is evidence in all three sources that the pact between the NUWSS and the Labour Party was very effective. Source 1 (a pamphlet published by the Election Fighting Fund in 1914) claims that the Election Fighting Fund is 'influencing the vote on which depends the fates of Governments.' There is some evidence for this in the sources. Source 1 claims that the Election Fighting Fund had a significant impact on party politics in Britain. The source states that 'The Liberal Party and the Conservative Party are today threatened by Labour.' This is partly supported by Source 3 (an extract from the annual report of the West Riding branch of the NUWSS, published in 1913) which shows that the NUWSS provided financial support to a Labour candidate in a by-election in 1913. Additionally, Sources 1 and 2 both indicate that the NUWSS had significant influence over the Labour Party. Source 1 states that 'workers will increasingly be associated with the political aims of women,' while Source 2 provides evidence of this influence in practice, referring to the NUWSS's success in explaining 'the real situation with regards to women's suffrage' to a member of the Labour Party. Source 2 is taken from the minutes of the Executive Committee of the Election Fighting Fund, 6 December 1912.

SOURCE 3

(Adapted from the annual report of the West Riding branch of the NUWSS, 1913. Mr Lunn was unsuccessful in the by-election of 1913)

The West Riding Federation had in its area the first by-election in which the Election Fighting Fund was brought into operation. We decided to support Mr Lunn, the Labour candidate, a convinced suffragist. We can look back on this important by-election with great satisfaction, for our speakers and workers undoubtedly made a great impression on the constituency.

The wider public debate

In addition to parliament and the suffrage movement, there was a widespread public debate about women's suffrage.

The media

Different newspapers took different positions on the question of suffrage:

- *The Times* consistently opposed women's suffrage. It tended to characterise suffragettes as hysterical women with too much free time.

- The *Illustrated London News* paid a lot of attention to suffragette protests. However this was because the protests were sensational and therefore helped to sell papers, not because the paper wanted to support women's rights.

- The *Manchester Guardian* supported women's suffrage but was critical of suffragette violence.

- The *Daily Herald*, founded by Labour MP George Lansbury, supported women's suffrage and claimed that suffragette violence was justified.

- The **satirical** magazine *Punch* supported women's suffrage and mocked Asquith for blocking women's rights.

Businesses

The suffragettes' own newspapers had a wide circulation amongst fashionable women. Therefore, stylish boutiques, such as Burberry, Swan & Edgar and Debenhams, bought advertising space in suffragette papers to sell their products to women.

Trade unions

Trade unions dominated by men tended to prioritise the rights of working men over those of women. For example, in 1901, the **Trades Union**

Congress stated that enfranchising working men was more important than enfranchising women. Some male trade unionists viewed the suffrage movement as middle class and out of touch with the needs of working people. However, over time, the trade unions became more sympathetic to women's suffrage due to:

- Increased female membership of trade unions. By 1905, trade unions for women boasted 70,000 members. In addition, by 1907, 15 per cent of British trade unions admitted both men and women.

- An EFF campaign to win the support for women's suffrage amongst male trade unionists. In February 1914, an EFF-organised mass rally at the Albert Hall was attended by members from a wide range of trade unions, and raised over £6000 for the suffrage campaign.

The anti-suffrage movement

Opposition to women's suffrage was formalised in 1908 with the creation of both the Women's National Anti-Suffrage League and the Men's Committee for Opposing Female Suffrage. In 1910, these organisations merged, creating the National League for Opposing Women's Suffrage. By 1914, the National League for Opposing Women's Suffrage had 50,000 female members.

These organisations campaigned in a similar way to the NUWSS by lobbying politicians, publishing pamphlets and propaganda, and organising petitions. Indeed, in 1908, the Women's National Anti-Suffrage League successfully organised a petition of 337,018 signatures against women's suffrage. This compared favourably to the suffragettes' petition of the same year, which collected only 288,736 signatures in favour of women's suffrage.

Christian groups

Group	Stance on women's suffrage
Church of England	• They had no official position on women's suffrage. • They condemned the militant actions of the suffragettes. • The Church Women's Suffrage League, established in 1913 to support women's suffrage, attracted 5,080 members in its first year.
Roman Catholic	• The majority of Catholics believed that women should not be involved in politics. • The Catholic Women's Suffrage Society was founded in 1911 and by 1913 it only had 1,000 members.

Below is a list of groups involved in the wider public debate about women's suffrage. Indicate the extent to which they supported women's suffrage by writing their numbers on the spectrum below. Write a sentence next to each to justify your placement.

1. The media
2. Businesses
3. The Church of England
4. The Catholic Church
5. Trades Union Congress
6. The anti-suffrage movement

Very supportive ←——————————————————————————————→ Openly hostile

Write the question

a

The following sources relate to the extent of trade union support for female suffrage in the period 1884–1914. Read the guidance detailing what you need to know about this topic. Having done this, write an exam-style part (b) question using the sources.

Use Sources 1, 2 and 3 and your own knowledge.

Do you agree with the view that...

_____

_____

SOURCE 1

(Adapted from Millicent Fawcett's Women's Suffrage: A Short History of a Great Movement, *published 1912)*

The Reform Bill of 1884 was not finally passed until late in the autumn. While the final stages of the measure were still pending the Trades Union Congress meeting passed a resolution, with only three dissenters, "That the Congress is strongly of the opinion that the franchise should be extended to women rate-payers." At that critical moment the working men's most powerful organisation stood by the women whom the Liberal Party had betrayed.

SOURCE 2

(Adapted from Jo Vellacott's From Liberal to Labour with Women's Suffrage, *published 1993)*

The Trades Union Congress met in September 1913. For some reason, and greatly to the NUWSS's dismay, there was initially no women's suffrage resolution on the agenda. But the women's friends at the Congress managed to get the issue debated as part of a discussion on electoral reform. A much stronger resolution condemning the Liberal Government's treatment of the franchise issue was also agreed by several unions. The miner's Union, however, decided not to give their support to the women's suffrage resolution.

SOURCE 3

(From Bob Whitfield The Extension of the Franchise, 1832–1931)*

When a resolution calling for the TUC to support women's suffrage was put to the annual congress in 1901, the trades union leaders quickly responded by adopting an alternative resolution in favour of full adult suffrage. Soon afterwards the Adult Suffrage Society was formed, led by the female trades unionist Margaret Bondfield; majority opinion within the Labour Party and the trades unions in the years before the outbreak of the First World War supported the extension of the franchise to all adults.

Representation of the People Act, 1918

Revised

Why was the Act passed?

The suffrage movement

The suffragettes kept women's rights at the top of the political agenda. Other contemporary issues, such as the government of Ireland, reform of the House of Lords, and the extension and defence of the British Empire threatened to divert attention away from the suffrage question. However, WSPU protests were so shocking (see page 28) that they kept the press focused on women's rights.

Suffragette campaigns forced politicians to address the issue of women's rights. However, suffragette violence alienated senior politicians, such as Lloyd George and Churchill. Therefore, senior politicians preferred to work with the moderate NUWSS. Indeed, the lobbying of the NUWSS played an equally important role in the sense that it put pressure on politicians to keep trying to reform the law.

Additionally, the patriotism of the WSPU and the NUWSS during the war won a great deal of political support for women's suffrage.

Limitations of the anti-suffrage movement

Conflicting opinions in the anti-suffrage movement limited its effectiveness. Male members such as Sir **Almroth Wright** stressed that women were too hysterical to be trusted with the vote. Female members such as **Mrs Humphry Ward** argued that women should be involved in politics, but that voting was not the best way for this to be achieved. Notably, the historian Martin Pugh has argued that the growth of the anti-suffrage movement was, in a sense, self-defeating as it proved that women were interested in politics and were able to engage in political debate.

The First World War

The First World War increased the scale of government, giving national government greater influence in the domestic sphere. For example, during the war, the government introduced some rationing of food. This further blurred the distinction between the 'separate spheres' (see page 4). Women contributed to war work (see page 62) and this gave politicians who had opposed women's suffrage, such as Asquith, an excuse to publicly endorse women's suffrage without losing pride.

Political changes during the war

The First World War resulted in a **coalition government** dominated by Liberals and Conservatives. In 1916, David Lloyd George replaced Herbert Asquith as Prime Minister. Lloyd George was sympathetic to women's suffrage.

The **Speaker's Conference** of 1916 recommended the enfranchisement of a limited number of women. The war also transformed debates about electoral advantage. The war created a consensus that all men, many of whom had fought for their country, deserved the right to vote. It was assumed that the new working-class voters would vote for the Liberals or for Labour. Consequently, enfranchising women over the age of 30 was justified as it was assumed they would vote Conservative, giving no party an obvious electoral advantage.

The international context

Britain was increasingly out of step with other democracies such as Australia, New Zealand, Finland and Norway who had all granted women the vote.

The Representation of the People Act, 1918

The 1918 Act extended the franchise to include all adult men over 21 and all women over the age of 30.

The significance of women's war work

It is sometimes argued that women were given the vote because they had proved themselves as workers during the First World War. This argument is difficult to sustain because the women who gained the vote in 1918 were over 30 whereas the majority of women working during the war were under 30.

RAG – Rate the timeline

Below are a sample part (b) exam-style question and a timeline. Read the question, study the timeline and, using three coloured pens, put a red, amber or green star next to the events to show:

- **Red:** Events and policies that have no relevance to the question
- **Amber:** Events and policies that have some significance to the question
- **Green:** Events and policies that are directly relevant to the question

1) Do you agree with the view that women's work in the First World War was the most significant reason for the passing of the Representation of the People Act in 1918?

Now repeat the activity with the following part (b) questions:

2) Do you agree with the view that between 1884 and 1914, the Liberal Party were wholly committed to advancing women's suffrage?

3) Do you agree with the view that by 1914 it was inevitable that women would be granted the vote?

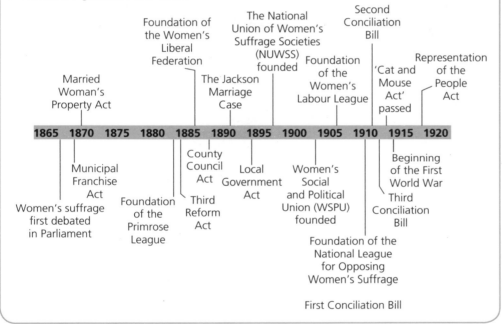

 Add own knowledge

Below is a sample part (b) question and to the right are two of three sources referred to in the question. In one colour, draw links between the sources to show ways in which they agree about the impact of women's work in the First World War. In another colour, draw links between the sources to show ways in which they disagree. Around the edge of the sources, write relevant own knowledge. Again, draw links to show the ways in which this agrees and disagrees with the sources.

Use Sources 1, 2 and 3 and your own knowledge.

Do you agree with the view that women's work in the First World War was the most significant reason for the passing of the Representation of the People Act in 1918?

SOURCE 1

(Adapted from Sandra Stanley Holton, Feminism and Democracy, *published 1986)*

Women's war work may have been important in converting some former opponents of women's suffrage, or providing others with a face-saving excuse to alter their positions. But even before this, the political alliances that the suffragists had formed in support of their demand had ensured that women would have to be granted the vote.

SOURCE 2

(Adapted from Arthur Marwick, War and Social Change in the Twentieth Century, *published 1974)*

The process by which women's participation in the war effort brought considerable political gains can be easily traced. What is most striking is the way in which the leading opponents of votes for women backed down, and declared that women had played a vital part in the national effort, and must be allowed to share in the politics of their country.

The female franchise and politics, 1918–1928

The impact of the Representation of the People Act (1918)

The impact on the electorate

The 1918 Act increased the total electorate from 7.7 million to 21.4 million, of which 43 per cent were women.

The impact on Parliament

The enfranchisement of women did not create significant change in the **gender** composition of Parliament (see table).

Women wanting to enter Parliament faced a series of obstacles:

Year of General Election	Number of female candidates	Number of women elected
1918	17	1
1922	33	5
1929	69	14

- Running for Parliament was expensive and few women could afford the costs.
- Political parties assumed that the electorate was not ready to vote for women and therefore only encouraged women to stand for election in seats that they knew would not be won by their party.

The impact on political parties

Labour established a Women's Section. This had special rights to elect women to senior Party committees such as the **National Executive Committee**. The Party employed Dr Marion Philips as Women's Organiser. She was tasked with increasing women's membership of the Party and increasing the number of female Labour voters.

The Conservatives encouraged middle-class women to participate in volunteer work for the Party. This was organised through the Primrose League and focused on raising money and persuading women to vote for the Party. In contrast, the Liberal Party did little to attract female support. The Women's National Liberal Federation designed a programme of legislation designed to appeal to women. However, Party leaders did little to promote this. Consequently, by 1928, the Liberal Party had only 100,000 female members, compared to the Labour Party's 300,000 and the Conservative Party's 1 million.

Legal change, 1918–1928

Between 1919 and 1928, the rights of women were advanced by a number of legal changes:

Date	Act	Details
1919	Repeal of the Sex Disqualification Act	Allowed women equal rights to become jurors, magistrates, barristers, and to graduate from the Universities of Oxford and Cambridge.
1922	Married Women's Maintenance Act	Gave married women abandoned by their husbands an allowance of 40 shillings plus 10 shillings per child.
1922	Infanticide Act	Recognised **post-natal depression** as an illness. Consequently, a woman who killed her new-born child whilst suffering from post-natal depression was charged with the lesser crime of **manslaughter** rather than murder.
1923	Matrimonial Causes Act	Gave women the same divorce rights as men.
1923	The Bastardy Act	Increased maintenance payments to single mothers.
1925	The Widows', Orphans and Old-Age Contributory Pensions Act	Gave widows the right to inherit their husband's pension.
1928	The Equal Franchise Act	Gave women over 21 the right to vote. In this sense, the Act ensured that women and men had the same political rights. The Conservatives were willing to equalise the franchise, in part because of the support they enjoyed from existing female voters. The percentage of the adult population who were able to vote rose from 74 per cent to 96.9 per cent.

Doing reliability well   (a)

Below are a series of definitions listing common reasons why sources are reliable or unreliable, and on this page a series of sources. Under each source, explain why the source is either reliable or unreliable for the purpose stated, justifying your answer by referring to the following definitions.

- **Vested interest:** the source is written so that the writer can protect their power or their financial interests.
- **Second-hand report:** the writer of the source is not an eyewitness, but is relying on someone else's account.
- **Expertise:** the source is written on a subject which the author (for example a historian) is an expert.
- **Political bias:** a source is written by someone with strong political views and reflects these views.
- **Reputation:** a source is written to protect the writer's reputation.

SOURCE 1

(Isabella Ford's letter to The Common Cause, *15 March 1918. The Common Cause was the magazine of the NUWSS)*

It is indeed wonderful when one wakes up in the morning to remember that now, at last, one is considered to be a real, complete human being! After thirty years of endeavour to make men understand they were only half the world we are filled with a deep and earnest thankfulness.

> The source is <u>reliable / fairly reliable / fairly unreliable/unreliable</u> as evidence of public feelings about the Representation of the People Act of 1918 because
>
> _____
>
> _____

SOURCE 2

(Adapted from a speech given by Herbert Asquith in Paisley in 1920)

There are about fifteen thousand women on the electoral register. They are dim and, for the most part, hopelessly ignorant of politics, flickering with gusts of emotion like a candle in the wind.

> The source is <u>reliable / fairly reliable / fairly unreliable/unreliable</u> as evidence of public feelings about the Representation of the People Act of 1918 because
>
> _____
>
> _____

SOURCE 3

(Adapted from Caroline Daley and Melanie Nolan, Suffrage and Beyond, *1994)*

The limited franchise given to women in 1918 was a clear indication of the fear that women would be in a majority in the electorate, and of a continuing doubt about whether women were as capable as men of exercising citizenship.

> The source is <u>reliable / fairly reliable / fairly unreliable/unreliable</u> as evidence of public feelings about the Representation of the People Act of 1918 because
>
> _____
>
> _____

Recommended reading

Below is a list of suggested further reading on this topic.

- Malcolm Pearce and Geoffrey Stewart, *British Political History 1867–1900,* pages 207–8, (1992)
- Constance Rover, *Women's Suffrage and Party Politics in Britain 1866–1914,* pages 170–8, (1967)
- K.D. Brown, *The First Labour Party 1906–14*, pages 233–51, (1985)

Exam focus

On pages 49–51 are sample answers to the exam-style questions on this page. Read the answers and the examiner comments around them.

(a) Study Sources 1, 2 and 3.

How far do the sources suggest that the British press were divided in their attitude to the campaigns of the suffrage movement in the years 1908–1913?

Explain your answer, using the evidence of Sources 1, 2 and 3. **(20 marks)**

(b) Use Sources 4, 5 and 6 and your own knowledge.

Do you agree with the view that the opposition of Herbert Asquith was the main reason why suffrage bills failed to be passed by Parliament in the years 1908–1914?

Explain your answer, using Sources 4, 5 and 6 and your own knowledge. **(40 marks)**

SOURCE 1

(From the Penny Illustrated Paper and Illustrated Times, *20 June 1908)*

The procession was remarkable not only for the exceptionally large number of women of all classes who marched in its ranks but also for the unusually numerous crowds of sightseers who thronged the whole of the route. "No man need have apologised for having a sister or an aunt in the procession" wrote one enthusiastic newspaper reporter. Personally, I would go even further, I would not have minded if I had had half a dozen sweethearts in the show. In fact I should have rather liked it.

SOURCE 2

(Adapted from an editorial published in The Economist *magazine 27 July 1912. The* Economist *magazine tended to support the Conservative Party)*

The average man and average woman think that window breaking and hunger striking merely show that the few who did it are unfit for politics. To succeed in politics you require a good temper and self-restraint, a respect for the law and a readiness to submit to the rule of the majority. Those who broke the law might be called hysterical by the public.

SOURCE 3

(From an editorial published in The Times, *16 March 1913)*

The suffragettes are regrettable by-products of our civilization, out with their hammers and their bags full of stones because of dreary, empty lives and high-strung, over-excitable natures.

SOURCE 4

(Adapted from Richard Toye, Lloyd George and Churchill: Rivals for Greatness, *published 2008)*

The key reason that women did not get the vote before 1918 was party politics. The Conservatives as well as the Liberals were divided on the issue. Balfour, for example, was in favour of votes for women, whereas Asquith was opposed. After 1906 a majority of MPs favoured some measure of female enfranchisement. What could not be agreed upon was which groups of women should be included. As Lloyd George and Churchill both came to see, any decision was likely to have an impact on future elections.

SOURCE 5

(Adapted from Constance Rover, Women's Suffrage and Party Politics in Britain 1866–1914, *published 1967)*

Asquith's attitude between 1908 and the end of 1911 was that although he was personally opposed to women's suffrage, it was a matter for the House of Commons to settle. At the end of 1911 he announced a government backed reform bill, which could be amended in favour of women. When the amendment was ruled out of order by the Speaker in early 1913, he promised time for a further private member's Bill. These continual postponements were more difficult for women than an outright refusal.

SOURCE 6

(Adapted from Emmeline Pankhurst, My Own Story, *published 1914)*

Winston Churchill attacked the Conciliation Bill because the class of women who would be enfranchised under it did not suit him.

When the vote was taken the Conciliation Bill had passed its second reading by a majority of 109. No measure during that Parliament had received so great a majority. The Bill could have been advanced to its final reading. However, Mr Asquith refused to allow any more time for the Bill during that session.

(a) Study Sources 1, 2 and 3.

How far do the sources suggest that the British press were divided in their attitude to the campaigns of the suffrage movement in the years 1908–1913?

Explain your answer, using the evidence of Sources 1, 2 and 3. **(20 marks)**

The three sources suggest a degree of unity between The Economist, in Source 2, and The Times, in Source 3. However, there is also disunity between Source 1, which is positive about the suffrage movement, and Sources 2 and 3, which criticise the suffrage campaigns.

Sources 2 and 3 are united in their rejection of the suffrage campaigns of 1912 and 1913. Both sources abhor suffragette militancy. Source 2 argues that 'window breaking and hunger striking merely show that the few who [do] it are unfit for politics.' Source 3 supports this when it argues that 'The suffragettes are regrettable by-products of our civilisation, out with their hammers and their bags full of stones.' The reference to hammers and stones is an implicit criticism of the window-breaking campaign referred to in Source 2. Sources 2 and 3 are also united in their condemnation of the motives behind violent campaigns, perhaps because they are both from right-wing publications. Source 2 argues that they are the result of hysteria. Source 3 agrees, arguing that suffragettes are campaigning because of their 'empty lives, and high-strung, over-excitable natures.' Therefore, Sources 2 and 3 suggest that sections of the British press were united in their dismissal of the campaigns of the suffrage movement.

However, Source 1 presents a very different picture of the suffrage campaigns. Whereas Source 2 and Source 3 stress violence, Source 1, quoting another newspaper, argues that 'no man need have apologised for having a sister or an aunt in the procession' implying that the march was respectable and therefore peaceful. There is also disagreement in the way that public reaction to the campaigns is reported. For example, Source 1 describes 'the unusually numerous crowd of sightseers who thronged the whole route.' However, Source 2 argues that the public feel the campaigners are 'hysterical'. Finally, there is a small disagreement within Source 1. The reporter quotes another newspaper, arguing that it does not go far enough in its praise of the suffrage campaign. Referring to the comment that 'No man need apologise for having a sister or an aunt in the procession,' he says 'Personally, I would go even further, I would not have minded if I had had half a dozen sweethearts in the show.' In this sense, the sources suggest that the press were divided about whether to support the suffrage campaign or not, and in the extent of their support.

In conclusion, Sources 1, 2 and 3 provide evidence that the British press was divided in their attitude to the campaigns of the suffrage movement in the years 1908–1913. Sources 2 and 3 are united in their criticism of the campaigns, whereas Source 1 is fulsome in its praise.

The introduction answers the question and summarises the position taken by the three sources.

This paragraph not only points out areas of agreement between Sources 2 and 3, but categorises these areas into those relating to the nature of the campaigns, and those relating to the motives behind them. This provides a clear structure to the paragraph, and ensures that the sources are compared as often as possible.

Here, reference is made to the provenance of the sources, but this is not developed to explain why the sources agree on the nature of the campaigns.

Here, the candidate notices that Source 1 quotes from another newspaper, so representing the views of two examples of the British press. This shows close reading of the source.

This paragraph would be an ideal place to analyse the reasons why Source 1 differs from Sources 2 and 3. For example, the candidate could mention that Source 1 is written in 1908, before the beginning of the violent campaigns, and that this could be the reason for its expression of sympathy. Furthermore, the candidate could state that Sources 2 and 3 are commenting on the campaign as a whole, whereas Source 1 describes only one protest.

15/20

The essay on page 49 gets a mark in Level 3. It selects relevant information from the sources, contains a detailed comparison of similarities and differences, and considers how far the sources suggest division in the British press. However, it does not get into Level 4 because it does not use the provenance of the sources to explain similarities and differences in their accounts.

(b) Use Sources 4, 5 and 6 and your own knowledge.

Do you agree with the view that the opposition of Herbert Asquith was the main reason why suffrage bills failed to be passed by Parliament in the years 1908–1914?

Explain your answer, using Sources 4, 5 and 6 and your own knowledge. **(40 marks)**

As Source 5 highlights, Herbert Asquith's opposition was one reason why suffrage bills failed to be passed by Parliament in the years 1908–1914. However, Asquith alone could not prevent the passage of a bill to enfranchise women. Electoral advantage also played a role, as noted in Sources 4 and 6, as did divisions with the major political parties, a point discussed in Source 4.

All of the sources agree that Asquith's opposition was a factor in the failure of suffrage bills in the period 1908–1914. Source 4 mentions that 'Asquith was opposed' to women's suffrage. Source 6 states that Asquith was responsible for the defeat of the Second Conciliation Bill, as 'Asquith refused to allow any more time' for the Bill to be passed by Parliament. In addition, Source 5 implies that Asquith was responsible for the failure of the 1912 Conciliation Bill. Asquith planned to introduce a 'reform bill, which could be amended in favour of women.' This was a tactic designed to distract politicians from the Third Conciliation Bill, ensuring that the Conciliation Bill failed. The Reform Bill also failed as the amendment that Asquith suggested was ruled 'out of order' by the Speaker of the House of Commons. Indeed, it seems that Asquith had anticipated that the Amendment would be rejected. Asquith's reluctance to support female suffrage was based on his belief that women could exert political influence through their husbands and fathers rather than through voting. In this way, Herbert Asquith's opposition to women's suffrage was one reason why a bill failed to pass in the period 1908–1914 because he used his influence as Prime Minister to defeat the Conciliation Bills and to undermine the Reform Bill.

Another reason why suffrage bills failed to pass Parliament between 1908 and 1914 was the issue of electoral advantage. Source 4 argues that one reason why bills failed to be passed was that there was no agreement about 'which groups of women should be included' in the franchise. This is because politicians realised that 'any decision was likely to have an impact on future elections.' Source 6 also recognises this problem. Emmeline Pankhurst writes 'Winston Churchill attacked the Conciliation Bill because the class of women who would be enfranchised under it did not suit him.' Source 4 notes that Lloyd George, like Churchill, was aware of the issue of electoral advantage.

This paragraph begins with some good cross-referencing using all three sources. This shows that the sources are being used in combination.

The second half of the paragraph contains some detailed own knowledge. However, there is very little integration between sources and own knowledge.

Electoral advantage was extremely significant following the 1910 election because it resulted in a hung Parliament where Liberals and Conservatives were equally matched. Any change to the electoral laws would have had an important effect on the outcome of future elections. Therefore, the Conservative Party favoured the enfranchisement of wealthy women, who were more likely to vote Conservative. The Liberal Party, by contrast, were in favour of enfranchising poorer voters, who were more likely to support them. In this way, electoral advantage was a key reason for the failure of suffrage bills because the Parties could not agree on exactly who should be enfranchised.

Here, the candidate introduces accurate and relevant own knowledge, placing the information from the sources in context.

A final reason why suffrage bills failed to pass Parliament between 1908 and 1914 was that the major political parties were divided amongst themselves over whether to grant women the vote. Source 4 notes that 'The Conservatives as well as the Liberals were divided on the issue.' For example, it argues that while Asquith was opposed to female enfranchisement, 'After 1906 a majority of MPs favoured some measure of female enfranchisement.' The Conservatives, for example, were sympathetic towards the enfranchisement of women because they hoped to gain some kind of electoral advantage. However, some such as the Conservative Lord Curzon, believed that women were too emotionally unstable to use their votes responsibly. In this way, the divisions within the major political parties caused suffrage bills to fail because they reduced the strength of support for suffrage legislation within Parliament.

This paragraph introduces another reason why suffrage bills failed in Parliament and therefore extends the range of the essay.

In conclusion, Asquith was one reason why suffrage bills failed to pass Parliament between 1908 and 1914. This is because he used his influence to prevent the passage of both the Conciliation Bills and the Reform Bill. However, Asquith was aided in the attempt by Lloyd George and Churchill who, aware of the political advantage reform might bring to their opponents, were also keen to block a suffrage bill. Additionally, the divisions within the political parties made the passage of a bill more difficult because there was no organised body of MPs to lend strength to a bill.

The conclusion is focused and summarises the argument of the essay, showing how the factors interrelate. However, the candidate does not use the sources to support their conclusion.

30/40

This essay gets a mark high in Level 3. The essay is focused on the question, shows good understanding of the sources, makes a range of relevant points, and uses a good deal of accurate supporting information. However, there is very little integration between the sources and own knowledge, and the conclusion is not based on an evaluation of the sources. Consequently, the essay cannot reach Level 4.

Moving from Level 3 to Level 4

The exam focus essays at the end of Sections 1 and 2 (pages 17–19 and 33–35) have been awarded Level 4. The essays here achieve a Level 3. Read all of the essays, and the examiner's comments provided. Make a list of the additional features required to push a Level 3 essay into Level 4, both for part (a) questions and part (b) questions.

Section 4: Changing educational and employment opportunities for women, 1870–1930

Education prior to 1870

Prior to 1870, working-class girls had access to free education from two sources: charities and factories.

From 1834, the government permitted the creation of workhouse schools, run by charities. By 1855, approximately 38,000 children were educated in workhouse schools. In addition, churches often ran schools.

From 1833, factories were required to educate the children that they employed. By 1860, approximately 80,000 children were being educated in factory schools.

Further reform

Date	Measure	Details
1870	Elementary Education Act	The 1870 Elementary Education Act introduced the following reforms: • It gave the government the power to establish schools where there was no existing provision. However, these schools could charge fees. • It provided funds to allow poor children to attend fee-paying schools. • It allowed the government to establish free schools in areas of poverty. • Education was made compulsory for all children aged five to thirteen, except where circumstances made attendance difficult, such as during harvest time when children were needed to work in the fields.
1880	Mundela Act	Made education compulsory for all children aged between five and ten regardless of circumstances.
1891	Elementary Education Act	Provided free school places for all children aged between five and ten.
1902	Education Act (Balfour's Act)	Merged the 2,568 school boards into 328 county council education authorities, with permission to establish secondary schools. These schools were either County High Schools, which were non-selective, or Grammar Schools, which selected students on the basis of academic ability.
1906	Education Act (Provision of Meals Act)	Gave local authorities permission to provide free school meals to the poorest students.
1907	Education Act (Administrative Procedures Act)	Gave the government the power to direct, regulate and inspect schools. Stated that a minimum of 25 per cent of secondary school places should be available free to the poorest students.

The impact of educational reform

The education acts of this period referred to the rights of 'children' to receive an education. Therefore, in legal terms, they treated girls and boys equally. In practice, however, some **gender** inequalities remained.

Evidence of equality

In 1851, 55 per cent of women were literate, compared to 70 per cent of men. By 1911, almost 100 per cent of men and women were literate.

By 1913, approximately half of grammar school students came from the working class, and approximately half of the working-class students were girls.

Evidence of inequality

Girls' education included compulsory **domestic science**, which re-emphasised the philosophy of 'separate spheres' (see page 4).

Co-educational schools tended to be segregated with separate entrances, playgrounds, departments and teachers for boys and girls.

Working-class girls were more likely to have female teachers. However, in 1914 only 59 per cent of female teachers were certified (i.e. qualified), compared to 88 per cent of male teachers.

Attendance rates for girls were poorer than those for boys, as girls were often required to stay at home to help with domestic chores.

Linking sources

Below are a sample part (a) question and the three sources referred to in the question. In one colour, draw links between the sources to show ways in which they agree about the impact of the Elementary Education Act of 1870 on attitudes towards the education of girls. In another colour, draw links between the sources to show ways in which they disagree.

Study Sources 1, 2 and 3.

How far do the sources suggest that the Elementary Education Act of 1870 changed attitudes to the education of girls in Britain?

SOURCE 1

(Adapted from the unpublished memoirs of Teresa Billington. She is recalling her time at Blackburn Convent School, a school she attended from 1884)

We were given a similar education to that of our grandmothers. We sat quietly in rows of desks and learned from books. We had long periods of religious instruction… Friday afternoon was devoted entirely to behaviour. 'Manners make the lady,' we were taught, 'not money or learning.' So we practised opening a door, entering and leaving a room, bringing in a letter, a message, a tray or a gift, and so on!

SOURCE 2

(From The Times, *28 November 1871)*

In a public meeting held in an infant school in Dulwich Mrs Grey, in a moving speech, affirmed that financial assistance for girls' schools was just as desirable as financial assistance for schools for boys. Referring to the Elementary Education Act, Mrs Grey pointed out that the provisions made under the Act were for girls as well as boys.

SOURCE 3

(From Hilda Martindale, From One Generation to Another, *published 1944)*

Lewes was a conservative town in those days, narrow in outlook both socially and religiously, and unfortunately not interested in education. My mother approved neither of the old-fashioned private schools nor of half-taught **governesses**. She tried hard to get a High School for Girls established in Lewes but was met with opposition on all sides. At Brighton there was such a school, so, in 1885, she decided to move there.

 Spot the inference **a**

High level answers avoid summarising or paraphrasing the sources, and instead make inferences from the sources. Below is a series of statements. Read Source 3 above and decide which of the statements:

- make inferences from the source (I)
- paraphrase the source (P)
- summarise the source (S)
- cannot be justified from the source (X).

Statement	I	P	S	X
Hilda Martindale's mother was unable to establish a girls' school in Lewes so she moved to Brighton, where there was a girls' school.				
Attitudes to the education of girls differed from place to place.				
The girls' school in Brighton had met with no opposition.				
People in Lewes were conservative in their social and religious outlook.				
Education provision for girls differed from place to place.				

The education of middle-class girls

Education prior to 1870

Prior to 1870, the majority of middle-class girls were educated at home by governesses. Home education focused on music, art and teaching young women to become wives and mothers.

Educational reformers

Mary Buss and Dorothea Beale were two important educational reformers during the Victorian period.

Mary Buss (1827–94)

Mary Buss was responsible for changing the focus of girls' education. She was determined that young women should get a broader education and learn more than just the skills necessary to be a good wife and mother.

Buss established the North London Collegiate School, a fee-paying school for girls, in 1850. It offered an education including Religious Studies, History, Geography, English Language and Literature, Maths, Political Economy, Gymnastics, German, Art and needlework. Additionally, Buss was only willing to employ qualified teachers who were specialists in the subjects they taught.

Buss was the headmistress of the North London Collegiate School from 1850 until 1894. During that time, she worked with **Emily Davies** (see page 56) to persuade educational authorities to allow girls to take public exams. As a result of her efforts, the Oxford and Cambridge Exam Board was established in 1873, offering public exams for girls and boys.

The North London Collegiate School became an example for other girls' schools, for example:

■ in 1871, Camden School opened
■ in 1881, the Perse School for Girls opened in Cambridge.

Buss worked hard to raise money to **endow** the schools so that bursaries were available for clever working-class girls.

Dorothea Beale (1831–1906)

Dorothea Beale was headmistress of Cheltenham Ladies' College. The school had been established in 1853, and Beale, who became headmistress in 1858, turned it into a prestigious boarding school for the daughters of the wealthiest people in Britain.

Under Beale, the College offered an education which mixed traditional subjects such as painting and music with a broader curriculum including English, Maths, Geography and Zoology.

The impact of Buss and Beale

The number of girls affected was small. By 1906, Cheltenham Ladies' College educated around 1,000 girls, and Camden School was of a similar size.

Buss and Beale proved that girls could cope with the pressure of exams and the pressure of academic subjects.

Buss and Beale's example led to the establishment of the Girls Public Day School Company in 1872 (known as the Girls Public Day School Trust from 1905) by Emily Shirreff and Mary Guerney. The Company set up local schools with parents as the **shareholders**. The schools were deliberately modelled on the North London Collegiate School. Headmistresses of the new schools were required to visit and study the North London Collegiate School before commencing employment. By 1898, the Girls Public Day School Company had set up 34 schools.

However, the impact of the Girls Public Day School Company was limited. Indeed, by 1900, 70 per cent of middle-class girls were educated at home.

How radical were the changes to the education of middle-class girls?

Schools for middle-class girls considerably increased the range of subjects that girls could study. They also prepared girls for higher academic study. However, neither Buss nor Beale fundamentally challenged the ideology of 'separate spheres' (see page 4). Indeed, Beale commented that her aim in improving education for girls was to create 'a wise woman who will be less likely to make a foolish marriage ... if girls were more accustomed to weigh and consider, there would be less extravagance and folly, better-ordered homes, children happier.'

Use the information on the opposite page to add detail to the mind map below.

Ways in which these reformers changed education for girls.

The Impact of Mary Buss and Dorothea Beale

Ways in which these reformers had a limited impact on education for girls.

 Write the question

The following sources relate to the effect of the reforms of Dorothea Beale and Mary Buss on the education of girls. Read the guidance detailing what you need to know about this topic. Having done this, write an exam-style part (b) question using the sources.

Use Sources 1, 2 and 3 and your own knowledge.

Do you agree with the view that...

_____

_____

SOURCE 1

(Adapted from Dale Spender and Elizabeth Sarah, Learning to Lose: sexism and education, *1980)*

Dorothea Beale did not seek to deviate from the Victorian feminine ideal, only to enhance it. Her pupils could look forward to a future of leisure and did not need to equip themselves for independence. Therefore the curriculum [at Cheltenham Ladies College] did not neglect traditionally female activities, and academic work was of a kind thought particularly appropriate to girls.

SOURCE 2

(Adapted from Dorothea Beale, Address to the National Association for the Promotion of Social Science, 1865)

And here let me at once say that I desire to institute no comparison between the mental abilities of boys and girls, but simply to describe what seems to be the right means of training girls so that they may best perform that submissive role to which I believe they have been called.

SOURCE 3

(Adapted from Sally Mitchell, Daily Life in Victorian England, *published in 1996)*

By the 1860s many middle-class parents understood that girls' education needed reform, and new academic schools were established. The first was North London Collegiate School, with Frances Mary Buss as headmistress. A 'collegiate' school had enough pupils to divide into separate classes by age and ability. By the 1890s the school's curriculum covered history, mathematics, French, German, Latin, biology, political economy, singing, drawing and gymnastics.

Women in higher education and the professions

Higher education

The establishment of schools and public exams for girls created a route from secondary to **higher education**. Indeed, in the Victorian period, several universities began to accept female students:

Date	University	Courses offered
1848	Queen's College, London	Teacher training Training for governesses
1849	Bedford College, London	Teacher training **Liberal arts**
1878	University of London Westfield College Royal Holloway	Degrees in all subjects

By 1900, various universities, including Manchester and Leeds, were awarding degrees to female students. However, Cambridge and Oxford, the most prestigious universities in Britain, still refused to grant degrees to women.

Cambridge and Oxford

Women at Cambridge

Cambridge University was reluctant to award degrees to women. Nonetheless, from the 1860s, there were signs of change:

- Due to the influence of Emily Davies, Henry Sidgwick, a **fellow** at Trinity College, began to organise lectures for women at Cambridge in 1869.
- The same year, Emily Davies established Girton College, a college for women only. This allowed female students to study at the university.
- In 1871, Henry Sidgwick and Millicent Fawcett founded a residential hall and library for women. This later became known as Newnham College.
- In 1877, 23 Cambridge lecturers agreed to allow women to attend their lectures.
- In 1884, all lectures were opened to women and women were allowed to sit university exams and gain certificates from the university. However, these were not degrees.
- Cambridge University only agreed to allow women to take degrees in 1947.

Women at Oxford

Oxford University was also reluctant to educate women. Efforts to include women in the university were divided along religious lines.

- **Anglicans** established Lady Margaret Hall in 1878. Women were allowed to live in the Hall and attend some university lectures.
- **Secular** campaigners established Somerville Hall in 1879.
- Oxford agreed to allow women to take degrees in 1920.

Women and professions

In the nineteenth century, it was necessary to have a degree in order to enter **professions** such as teaching, law and medicine.

Teaching

Teaching was the profession most open to women. Indeed, the increasing number of female students led to an increasing demand for female teachers. Moreover, teaching was viewed as a caring and nurturing profession and so fitted with the notion of 'separate spheres' (see page 4).

Law

Legally, women were excluded from practising law. However, there were two high-profile women lawyers during this period.

Cornelia Sorabji was born in Nashik in India in 1866 and adopted by British missionary parents. She studied at Somerville College in Oxford, and in 1892 obtained special permission to take a degree in Civil Law.

Helena Normanton was a lecturer at Glasgow University. She applied to study law at the **Middle Temple** in 1918. However, she was rejected. Nonetheless, she was admitted to Middle Temple at the end of 1919 and was **called to the Bar** in 1922. She became the first woman barrister to practise at the High Court of Justice and the Central Criminal Court.

The exclusion of women from the legal profession was removed in 1919.

Medicine

Women were allowed to practise medicine following the 1876 Enabling Act which opened all medical colleges to women. Prior to this, Elizabeth Blackwell and Elizabeth Garrett Anderson were able to register as doctors due to loopholes in the system.

Highlighting integration

Below are a sample part (a) question and two paragraphs written in answer to this question. Read the question and the two answers, as well as the sources. Then, using a highlighter, highlight examples of integration – where sources are used together. You cannot reach Level 3 or Level 4 of the part (a) mark scheme (see page 77) without integration of the sources. Which paragraph reaches the higher level?

Study Sources 1, 2 and 3.

How far do the sources agree that it was with reluctance that Cambridge University admitted female students in the period 1896–1922?

> Source 1 argues that allowing women to study at the university would 'harm the University's reputation as a place dedicated to the education of men.' Source 2 argues that the presence of women in lectures stopped men learning. It states 'their presence in classes prevents men from speaking freely.' Source 3 states that it is 'neither possible nor desirable' to increase the number of women at the university. In this way, all three sources suggest that Cambridge University was reluctant to admit female students.

> There is evidence in all three sources that Cambridge University was reluctant to admit female students. Sources 1 and 2 argue that women had a damaging effect on university life. For example, Source 1 argues that allowing women to study at the university would 'harm the University's reputation as a place dedicated to the education of men.' Similarly, Source 2 argues that the presence of women in lectures stopped men learning. It states 'their presence in classes prevents men from speaking freely.' Source 3 is more positive about the impact of women. Nevertheless, it is cautious about increasing their numbers. It states that it is 'neither possible nor desirable' to increase the number of women at the university. Source 3 may be more positive than Sources 1 and 2 because it is written in 1922, almost 30 years after Sources 1 and 2, and after women had been involved in the University for a substantial period of time.

SOURCE 1

(From The Times, *14 March 1896)*

The committee opposed to the granting of BA degrees from Cambridge University to women have published the following statement signed by 2,088 members of the governing body of the University:

'The admission of women to the University would be nothing less than a revolution and would bring about consequences that would harm the University's reputation as a place dedicated to the education of men.'

SOURCE 2

(Adapted from a private letter written by Alfred Marshall, Professor of Political Economy at Cambridge University, 15 October 1896)

When lecturing to women alone I have adopted a different manner of teaching which I believe is better adapted for them. Their presence in classes with men prevents men from speaking freely either in asking or answering questions.

SOURCE 3

(Adapted from a report produced by the Royal Commission on the Universities of Oxford and Cambridge, 1922)

Although we think it neither possible nor desirable to increase the number of women at Cambridge, it is, in our opinion, of great importance that Cambridge should continue to be a centre of the highest education for women. The advantages which women obtain from the intellectual atmosphere of the university are very great. It is highly desirable that a limited number of able women should continue to be trained at Cambridge.

Legislation and the lives of working women

Women at work, 1851–1901

Between 1851 and 1901, the proportion of women in employment remained stable, forming approximately 30 per cent of the workforce. Nonetheless, industrialisation brought about important shifts in the employment of women:

- The number of women employed in agriculture declined.
- The number of women employed in the service industry, in domestic service, and in the professions, increased.

Workplace legislation

From the 1840s, Parliament passed legislation which aimed to improve conditions in Britain's factories. This legislation did not focus specifically on women in the workplace, but did have an impact on their lives.

Date	Act	Provisions
1867	Agricultural Gangs Act	Prevented the employment of children under the age of eight in **agricultural gangs**. Farmers employing children were required to employ a female supervisor. Women could only be employed in all-female agricultural gangs.
1874	Factory Act	Introduced a maximum nine-hour working day for women and children. Increased the age of full-time work from thirteen to fourteen. Increased the age at which children could work in factories from eight to ten.
1878	Factory and Workshop Act	Outlawed overcrowding and poor ventilation in factories.
1886	Shop Hours Regulation Act	Introduced a maximum 74-hour working week for children.
1891	Factory Act	Increased the age at which children could work in factories from ten to eleven. Outlawed the employment of women in the four weeks after they had given birth.
1896	Truck Act	Outlawed **payment in kind**.
1901	Factory Act	Increased the age at which children could work in factories from eleven to twelve. Introduced a maximum eight-hour working day for women.
1911	Shops Act	Required all shops to close for half a day every week.

Enforcement

These laws were enforced by the government. However, enforcement was not uniform. In this sense, while the laws changed the **de jure** position of women and children, they did not always bring about **de facto** change.

The impact of the acts

Laws relating to employment were difficult to enforce for the following reasons:

- Often laws were vague. For example, the 1878 Factory and Workshop Act did not specify what constituted 'overcrowding' or 'proper ventilation'.
- New laws often required the employment of a Lady Factory Inspector. Lady Factory Inspectors were usually middle-class women who did not understand the lives of the working class and found it difficult to interact with them. Therefore, working-class women often colluded with their factory bosses to cover up illegal practices.
- Women themselves attempted to evade the new laws. For example, many women could not afford to lose income and so refused to reveal the fact that they had just given birth. Consequently, they made no use of the 1891 Factory Act which prohibited an early return to work.
- Some of the Acts, including the 1886 Shop Hours Regulation Act, did not give the government the power or means to enforce the provisions of the Act. Therefore, they could only be enforced if individual workers went to court. Court cases were expensive and so individuals could not afford to do this.
- In spite of these problems, the Acts brought about some change in the lives of working women. For example, the 1911 Shops Act did lead to a reduction in the working week.

Spectrum of significance

Below is a list of factors that brought about change in the lives of women in the late nineteenth century. Indicate the extent to which they improved opportunities for women by writing their numbers on the spectrum below. Having done this, write a brief justification of your placement, explaining why some of these factors are more important than others.

1. Legal educational reform.
2. The reforms of Mary Buss and Dorothea Beale.
3. The establishment of universities for women.
4. The decision to allow women to study at the Universities of Cambridge and Oxford.
5. Opportunities for women to practise professions.
6. Workplace legislation.

←——→

Great improvement   No improvement

Add own knowledge

Below are a sample part (b) question and the three sources referred to in the question. In one colour, draw links between the sources to show ways in which they agree about the impact of workplace legislation on opportunities for women. In another colour, draw links between the sources to show ways in which they disagree. Around the edge of the sources, write relevant own knowledge. Again, draw links to show the ways in which this agrees and disagrees with the sources.

Use Sources 1, 2 and 3 and your own knowledge.

Do you agree with the view that workplace legislation in the period 1867–1911 improved opportunities for women? Explain your answer, using Sources 1, 2 and 3 and your own knowledge.

SOURCE 1

(Adapted from Sonya O. Rose, Limited Livelihoods: Gender and Class in Nineteenth-Century England, *published 1993)*

In 1874 Parliament passed the Factories Bill that limited women's work in textile factories. The debates about this law focused on the problem of 'the working mother' and reinforced a particular view of who was responsible for looking after children.

SOURCE 2

(Adapted from Mary Lyndon Shanley, Feminism, Marriage, and Law in Victorian England, *published 1993)*

The main Parliamentary opponent to labour legislation was Henry Fawcett [the husband of Millicent Fawcett]. He opposed any legal restrictions on the hours women might work. To limit the hours of women and not of men suggested that women, like children, were not able to make their own decisions. Outside Parliament, others opposed regulation because they insisted that women must be regarded as being equally competent and independent as men.

SOURCE 3

(Adapted from Beatrice Webb, Women and the Factory Acts, *published 1896)*

It is frequently stated that any laws which limit women's work will limit their employment opportunities. If employers are not allowed to make their women work overtime, they will, it is said, prefer to have men. But this conclusion rests on the assumption that men and women are competing for the same employment. This is very far from being the case. In over nine-tenths of industrial work there is no such thing as competition between men and women: the men do one thing, and the women do another. There is no more chance of having our houses built by women than of getting our floor scrubbed by men.

Trade unions and technology

Women and trade unions

The leaders of trade unions were not entirely happy about women entering the workplace. They had the following concerns:

- Women were paid less than men. Consequently, they were concerned that men would be made redundant so that women could be employed.
- Some believed that a woman's place was in the home.
- Some believed that women's rights were a distraction from the union's central focus: the pay and conditions of working men.
- Many believed that women would inevitably leave work to become mothers.

The unionisation of women

There were three main ways in which women could participate in unions:

- Some unions, such as the National Union of Clerks, admitted men and women on equal terms.
- Some unions had 'women's sections'.
- Some unions only admitted women.

The number of unionised female workers increased in the early twentieth century. In 1906, there were 167,000 women in unions, mostly in the textile industry; by 1914, that figure had risen to 358,000. However, they formed only a small proportion of the total female workforce. For example, in 1910, out of 22,000 female shop assistants, only 2,000 were members of the National Union of Shop Assistants. Additionally, women formed only a small proportion of the total unionised workforce. For example, in 1918, there were 5.3 million men in unions, compared to only 1.2 million women.

The Women's Trade Union League

The Women's Trade Union League was founded by Emma Patterson in 1875. The Union represented traditionally female industries such as dress-makers, upholsterers, book-binders, jam-makers, shop assistants and typists. In 1906, the Women's Trade Union League had 211,000 members out of a total female workforce of 5 million.

The National Federation of Women Workers

The National Federation of Women Workers was founded in 1906. In contrast to the Women's Trade Union League, it attempted to provide one trade union for all women regardless of their job. It attempted to attract members by having low membership fees. Unlike the Women's Trade Union League it had a **strike fund**. In 1907, it had 2,000 members, and by 1914 it had 20,000 members.

Technology in the workplace

Technological innovation had an impact on working women, particularly those in the middle class. For example, during the 1880s, typewriters were introduced into the workplace. They were seen as a 'female tool' and typing was likened to playing a musical instrument. The telephone and **telegraph** also became widespread in the workplace during the 1880s.

The combination of typewriter, telephone and telegraph created a new secretarial role combining typing, **shorthand** and administration. This role appealed to middle-class women because it was clerical rather than manual, and the workplace was hygienic. In 1881, the Civil Service established the role of 'women clerks'. Later, in the 1890s, it created the role of 'female assistant'. By 1914, the Post Office had become the largest employer of middle-class women. Many of these women were employed as 'female sorters', a job created in 1883 requiring women to sort the mail.

Below are a sample part (a) exam-style question, the sources referred to in the question, and a paragraph written in answer to this question. Read the paragraph and identify parts of the paragraph that are not directly relevant to the question. Draw a line through the information that is irrelevant and justify your deletions in the margin.

Study Sources 1, 2 and 3.

How do the sources suggest that the trade union movement 'did a great favour to the cause of the woman worker' (Source 3)?

> There is evidence in all three sources that suggests that trade union did, as Source 3 claims, 'a great favour to the cause of the woman worker.' All three sources were written between 1875 and 1925, a period when many women were joining unions. Sources 1, 2 and 3 agree that women are exploited by employers. Source 1 claims that 'women need protection,' while Source 2 refers to women workers paid on '8 shillings a week.' Similarly, Source 3 objects to 'starvation wages and intolerable conditions.' All three sources make these statements to underline the benefits for women of joining a union. Sources 2 and 3 provide evidence of the support provided by unions. Source 3 was written after Source 2. Source 2 contrasts wages of unionised and non-unionised women, claiming that unionised women earn '30 shillings a week.' Similarly, Source 3 argues that 'the strike among women employed at Millwall Food Preserving Factory would have been doomed to failure' without the support of the National Federation of Women Workers. The National Federation of Women Workers was founded in 1906, and by 1907 it had 2,000 members.

SOURCE 3

(Adapted from an editorial in Time and Tide, *27 February 1925.* Time and Tide *was a weekly magazine, supportive of women's rights and the rights of workers)*

The National Federation of Women Workers did a great favour to the cause of the woman worker. Without the support of this organisation, the strike among women employed at Millwall Food Preserving Factory would have been doomed to failure. Relief from their starvation wages and intolerable conditions was largely due to the National Federation of Women Workers.

On page 15 are a series of definitions listing common reasons why sources are reliable or unreliable. Read Sources 1 and 2 above. Below, explain why each source is either reliable or unreliable for the purpose stated, justifying your answer by referring to the definitions: Vested interest, Second-hand report, Expertise, Political bias, Reputation.

> Source 1 is <u>reliable / unreliable</u> as a description of public attitudes to the unionisation of women because
>
> _____

> Source 2 is <u>reliable / unreliable</u> as a description of the impact of the unionisation of women because
>
> _____

SOURCE 1

(Adapted from George Howell, The Conflicts of Capital and Labour, *published 1878. George Howell was a Trade Union leader. Here, he is explaining why women should be admitted to trade unions)*

Women are essentially weak. Some of the causes of this weakness lie deep and hidden in human nature, others are not difficult to find. The fact, however, is clear: women need protection.

SOURCE 2

(Adapted from The Times, *28 December 1907)*

Last night a meeting was called by the National Federation of Women Workers. Mr W. C. A. Anderson said that the purpose of the meeting was to impress on women the importance of joining the union. He said he knew some industries in which females were earning 30 shillings a week, but it was only because they belonged to a strong union. It was terrible that women should be expected to work for 8 shillings a week.

Women's work in the First World War

The impact of the war on women's employment

Initially, businesses and the middle classes believed that the First World War would lead to an economic recession. Therefore, businesses laid off workers, and middle-class families terminated the employment of their domestic servants. Consequently, by September 1914, 190,000 women had lost their jobs. In response, the Queen's Work for Women Fund was established in 1914 to retrain women to produce war goods.

Women and munitions work

The large demand for war goods led to massive demand for female workers in factories. Consequently, the government began a propaganda campaign to enlist women in the munitions industry. Also, in March 1915, the government worked with the NUWSS (see page 26) to establish the Women's War Register which aimed to match skilled women to job vacancies. Within two weeks, 33,000 women had signed up to the Register, and in the following months that number increased to 100,000.

Munitions factories

Munitions production included the production of metals, chemicals, weapons, ammunition, uniforms, clothes, processed foods and tents. Some munitions production was organised directly by the government, while some took place in privately owned factories. The number of women employed in production rose throughout the war:

	Mining	Metals	Chemicals
1914	7,000	170,000	40,000
1915	6,500	203,000	48,000
1916	11,000	370,000	87,000
1917	12,000	523,000	109,000
1918	13,000	594,000	104,000

Public Record Office, MUN 5/7/1/324/34. Figures taken from diagrams based on Section C of the employment report prepared by the Board of Trade in January 1919.

Women and unions during the war

The Women's war Interest Committee, established to promote women's employment rights during the war, advised women to join unions. Indeed, there was a growth in female union membership during the war, from 358,000 in 1914 to 1.2 million in 1918. Nonetheless, traditional unions were concerned over three issues: dilution, substitution and equal pay.

Dilution

Many unions believed that employing women threatened the pay and status of male workers. Consequently, they only agreed to the employment of women if skilled jobs were 'diluted'. By this they meant that a single skilled job would be broken down and simplified so that it could be performed by several unskilled female workers. In this sense, women would be employed in lower status and lower paid jobs than the men they replaced. Unions also demanded that men would be rehired to their original jobs following the war.

Substitution

Unions were also concerned about substitution – the practice of directly replacing a male worker with a female worker. Unions agreed to substitution on the basis that men would be re-employed once the war was over.

Equal pay

On average, women were paid a third less than men doing similar jobs:

- Dilution resulted in several women being paid fractions of a skilled man's salary.
- In 1916, women employed in government clerical work earned only 20 shillings per week, when the men they had replaced had earned 40 shillings.
- In 1917, the Committee on Production increased the pay of men in munitions factories, but not that of women.
- In 1917, the Agricultural Wages Board agreed a weekly wage of 25 shillings for men, but only 18 shillings for women.

Unions responded to the lack of equal pay in a variety of ways. The National Union of Clerks campaigned for equal pay, whereas unions such as the Amalgamated Society of Engineers refused to admit women members of campaign for equal pay.

Explain the difference
(a)

Sources 1 and 2 give different accounts of women's work during the First World War. List the ways in which the sources differ. Explain the differences between the sources using the provenance of the sources alone. The provenance appears at the top of the source in brackets.

SOURCE 1

(Adapted from a report by the Chief Factory Inspector published in early 1916)

In many industries, remarkable figures are given as to output of women in jobs from which they were previously excluded. There is in progress a 'breaking up of old superstitions' as regards division of labour.

SOURCE 2

(Adapted from the Report of the War Cabinet Committee on Women in Industry, 1919)

The Engineering and National Employers' Federation submitted the following statement about the comparative quality and quantity of men's and women's output:

Quality

Sheet Metal – Better than men's work

Engineering – Women's work equal to boys. Men's far superior.

Shells – Men, then boys, women last.

Quantity

Sheet Metal – Women 90 per cent of men's output

Engineering – Approximately two-thirds of men

Shells – Boys, then men, women last.

Write the question
 (a)

Sources 1–3 relate to women's work in the First World War. Read the guidance detailing what you need to know about this topic. Having done this, write an exam-style part (a) question using the sources.

Study Sources 1, 2 and 3.

How far does the evidence of Sources 1, 2 and 3 agree with the view that...

_____

_____

SOURCE 3

(Adapted from The East Grinstead Observer, *17 June 1916. The newspaper is describing the report of Miss Bradley, agricultural organising officer for the Board of Trade)*

She said that women had responded splendidly to the call for workers in agriculture. However, the farmers felt differently, but she realised that there were difficulties and prejudices which were being gradually overcome and that when farmers realised that women could do useful work they would accept their service more, and more readily. Women were proving in many directions that they could perform useful work – in offices, in munitions works, and repairing roads. On farms, too, they could be of great assistance as they could do valuable work with weeding.

Job opportunities in the 1920s

Employment after the war

The First World War played a major role in breaking down the 'separate spheres' philosophy (see page 4). Nonetheless, at the end of the war, there was no clear consensus on the appropriate role for women.

Declining women's employment

Following the war, five factors played a role in reducing female employment:

■ Victory on the Western Front meant there was no longer demand for munitions, and therefore female munitions workers were **laid off**.

■ At the end of the war, around 3.5 million men were **demobilised** and returned to work. Unions, the government, and employers expected women to give up their jobs to returning soldiers.

■ The **economic recession** that followed the war also played a role in forcing women out of the labour force. Employers could not afford to expand their workforce, and gave men priority when offering employment.

■ The Restoration of Pre-War Practices Act (1919) ordered all 'dilutees' to be replaced by skilled workers – men returning from the war.

■ The reorganisation of the Civil Service in 1919 led to large numbers of female workers being replaced by male workers.

■ By the end of 1919, 750,000 women had left the workforce.

Government action

In spite of the declining female workforce, in 1919, the government took two steps to support women workers (see table).

Women's work in the 1920s

During the 1920s, women were predominantly employed in the following areas of employment:

Area of employment:	Percentage of working women employed in this area:
Domestic service	56
Clerks and typists	10
Textile workers	23
Other	11

In addition, changes in manufacturing processes brought new opportunities for women. Women were employed on production lines producing goods such as radios, watches and silver-plated cutlery.

Married women faced discrimination, as it was widely believed that the husband was the breadwinner for the household. Indeed, during 1921 and 1922 London County Council laid off all married women teachers. This **marriage bar** would not be lifted until 1935.

Overall, there was little increase in women's employment in the 1920s. According to census data, around 34 per cent of women were in work in 1911. By 1921 this had dipped to 32 per cent, and by 1931, it had returned to 34 per cent.

During the 1920s, there was a small increase in the relative pay of women. In 1900, women earned, on average, 44 per cent of male average earnings. By the early 1930s, this figure had risen to 48 per cent.

Government action	Benefits	Limitations
Sex Disqualification (Removal) Act	• Removed barriers to women entering the professions. • By 1922, there were 77 female barristers. • The proportion of female doctors rose from 6 per cent in 1914 to 7.4 per cent in 1925.	• The act did little to benefit working-class women who did not have access to the education required to enter the professions.
Unemployment benefit for women	• The government provided 25 shillings per week to women who registered as 'unemployed'.	• The amount of money provided by the government decreased over time, and by the end of 1919 was only 15 shillings per week. • Women were denied the benefit if they refused to work as domestic servants. The average weekly wage for a domestic servant was only 6 shillings per week. • In March 1919, 494,000 women claimed the benefit. Following media attacks on women 'scroungers', the number decreased to 29,000 by 1920.

RAG – Rate the line

Below are a sample part (b) exam-style question and a timeline. Read the question, study the timeline and, using three coloured pens, put a red, amber or green star next to the events to show:

- **Red:** Events and policies that have no relevance to the question
- **Amber:** Events and policies that have some significance to the question
- **Green:** Events and policies that are directly relevant to the question

1) Do you agree with the view that opportunities for women in the workplace increased in the period 1870–1928?

Now repeat the activity with the following part (b) questions:

2) Do you agree with the view that middle-class women were the main beneficiaries of educational and workplace reform in the period 1870–1928?

3) Do you agree with the view that the philosophy of 'separate spheres' was challenged in the period 1900–1928?

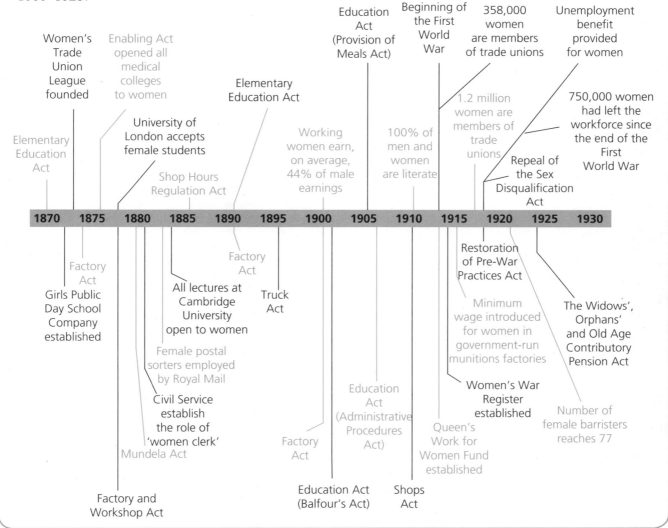

Recommended reading

Below is a list of suggested further reading on this topic.

- Paula Bartley, *Votes for Women 1860–1928*, pages 144–7, (2007)
- Harold L. Smith, *British Feminism in the Early Twentieth Century*, pages 53–62, (1990)
- Cheryl Law, *Suffrage and Power: The Women's Movement 1918–28*, pages 66–88, (1997)

Exam focus

On pages 67–69 are sample answers to the exam-style questions on this page. Read the answers and the examiner comments around them.

(a) Study Sources 1, 2 and 3.

How far do the sources suggest that the creation of the Girls Public Day School Company allowed middle-class girls the same educational opportunities as middle-class boys?

Explain your answer, using the evidence of Sources 1, 2 and 3. **(20 marks)**

(b) Use Sources 4, 5 and 6 and your own knowledge.

Do you agree with the view that Trades Unions failed to support women in the workplace in the period 1875–1918?

Explain your answer, using Sources 4, 5 and 6 and your own knowledge. **(40 marks)**

SOURCE 1

(Adapted from Dorothea Beale, Address to the National Association for the Promotion of Social Science, *published 1865)*

And here let me at once say that I desire to institute no comparison between the mental abilities of boys and girls, but simply to describe what seems to be the right means of training girls so that they may best perform that submissive role to which I believe they have been called.

SOURCE 2

(Adapted from the Belfast Newsletter, *30 May 1872)*

It is pleasant to report the proposal to establish a Girls' Public Day-School on the model of Cheltenham College for Boys, where a thorough education shall be given, at a modest cost. The teachers will be ladies, who will be so highly paid as to attract the most qualified staff. Nothing will be done but in the very best way, and on the most approved methods.

SOURCE 3

(Adapted from Vera Brittain, Testament of Youth, *1933. Brittain is recalling her education at the turn of the twentieth century)*

In those days, girls' private schools attracted only a few parents who wished to train their daughters for careers. Both for the young women and their mothers, the occurrence that loomed largest on the horizon was marriage, and almost every girl left school with the ambition to get engaged before everybody else.

SOURCE 4

(Adapted from a speech by Harry Broadhurst given to the Trades Union Congress (TUC) in 1877)

It is their duty as men and husbands to use their utmost efforts to bring about a situation where their wives should be in their proper sphere at home instead of being dragged into competition for jobs against the great and strong men of the world.

SOURCE 5

(Adapted from Claire A. Culleton, Working Class Culture, Women, and Britain, 1914–1921, *published 2000)*

Most working-class women's salaries before the First World War were so low that they were unable to join unions because they were unable or unwilling to pay the necessary dues. Improvements in women's salaries by 1914 helped to increase the number of women in trade unions, which tripled during the war, rising to 1,342,000 by 1920.

SOURCE 6

(Adapted from Elizabeth Roberts, Women's Work, 1840–1940, *published 1995)*

The last quarter of the nineteenth century saw active female involvement in trade unionism through the creation of all-female unions. However, their leaders were not from the working class and it has been suggested they did not always represent what working class women themselves wanted. The women's trade union movement was dominated by middle-class women for many years.

(a) Study Sources 1, 2 and 3.

How far do the sources suggest that the creation of the Girls Public Day School Company allowed middle-class girls the same educational opportunities as middle-class boys?

Explain your answer, using the evidence of Sources 1, 2 and 3. **(20 marks)**

Taken together, the three sources suggest that the creation of the Girls Public Day School Company allowed middle-class girls the same educational opportunities as middle-class boys to some extent. However, it is important to distinguish between the educational opportunities, discussed particularly in Source 2, and the outcomes of girls' education, which is the focus of Sources 1 and 3.

Sources 1 and 3 agree that girls' education at the Girls' Public Day Schools was primary focused on producing good wives. In this sense, they suggest that girls in these schools had different educational opportunities to boys, as boys were being prepared for careers rather than domestic duties. For example, Source 3 says that 'for young women and their mothers, the occurrence that loomed largest on the horizon was marriage.' Source 1 supports this, as Dorothea Beale states explicitly that her schools were designed to equip young women for 'that submissive role to which I believe they have been called.' This is a reference to women's role within marriage. Equally, Source 2 acknowledges that the teachers at Girls' Public Day Schools 'will be ladies', and female teachers were likely to be less well-qualified than male teachers in the late Victorian period. Source 1 also makes reference to the natural abilities of boys and girls. Beale states that she desires 'to institute no comparison between the mental abilities of boys and girls.' This could be an acknowledgement that boys and girls are so different that a comparison would be unhelpful. In this sense, Beale could be acknowledging that her schools have no need to offer girls the same educational opportunities as boys. However, it could also be a reference to her reluctance to engage in a debate about different mental abilities. Clearly, the focus on producing good wives and the fact that girls would be taught by female teachers indicates that middle-class girls did not receive the same educational opportunities as middle-class boys in all respects.

Source 2, on the other hand, stresses the similarity between Belfast's Girls' Public Day School and Cheltenham College for Boys. Indeed, it explicitly states that the girls' school would be established 'on the model of Cheltenham College for Boys.' Additionally, Source 2 argues that girls attending the Belfast School will be taught by 'the most qualified staff' and by the 'most approved methods.' In this sense, the curriculum was modelled on the best examples of boys' education. Furthermore, it should be noted that the emphasis on marriage in Sources 1 and 3 does not imply that school life would be different for girls and boys. Moreover, the fact that Dorothea Beale is speaking about female education to the National Association for the Promotion of Social Sciences is an indication that she herself had been involved in promoting learning for girls, specifically extending the curriculum for girls to include social sciences. Clearly, although the focus was still very much on preparing girls for marriage, Girls' Public Day Schools did this in the broadest possible way, offering a similar curriculum to the best boys' schools.

In conclusion, the sources clearly suggest that the creation of the Girls' Public Day School Company did little to bring the aspirations of young women in line with those of young men. Nonetheless, in terms of the curriculum available, there is a strong suggestion that the Girls' Public Day Schools did allow middle-class girls similar educational opportunities to middle-class boys.

The introduction distinguishes between educational opportunities and educational outcomes in order to consider how far the sources point to sexual equality in education.

This paragraph immediately highlights a similarity between Sources 1 and 3, and therefore begins the essay with clear comparison.

The candidate begins this paragraph with the best evidence available in the sources that there were equal educational opportunities for boys and girls.

The essay does not recognise that Source 2 only describes *proposals* and only for one school. This evidence is important as it could be the cause of the differences between Source 2 and Sources 1 and 3.

The conclusion is consistent with the introduction and uses the distinction between the outcomes of education and the opportunities in schools to consider how far middle-class girls and boys had the same educational opportunities.

17/20

The essay on page 67 gets a mark in Level 4 because it contains a detailed comparison of the sources, with a strong focus on the question. What is more, the distinction between the outcomes of education and educational opportunities themselves is sustained throughout the essay. The provenance of Source 1 is also used to demonstrate a similarity between the curriculum outlined in Source 2 and the curriculum of Dorothea Beale's school. However, the essay does not get into the highest part of Level 4 because it does not recognise that Source 2 may differ from Sources 1 and 3 because it only provides evidence relating to one school.

(b) Use Sources 4, 5 and 6 and your own knowledge.

Do you agree with the view that Trades Unions failed to support women in the workplace in the period 1875–1918?

Explain your answer, using Source 4, 5 and 6 and your own knowledge. (40 marks)

Trades Unions failed to support women in the workplace particularly at the beginning of the period, as indicated by Source 4. However, as Sources 5 and 6 acknowledge, there was change over time, and by the beginning of the First World War, the example of all-female Unions, increasing female membership, and a greater awareness of the rights of women, meant that unions were better at fighting for women's rights. Nonetheless, unions did fail women during the war over issues such as dilution and substitution.

Trade Unions failed women in three ways. First, trade unions tended to have a conservative view of the role of women. This is obvious from Source 4, which argues that it is the duty of 'men and husbands to use their utmost efforts to bring about a situation where their wives should be in their proper sphere at home.' Unions, especially in the early part of the period, did not welcome women because they felt that women belonged at home, that men's rights in the workplace were more important than women's, and because, as women would become mothers, they would only work for a small part of their lives. Additionally, Source 4 points to a further reason why unions failed women. Source 4 mentioned 'competition for jobs' between men and women. Women were cheaper to employ than men and unions feared that employing women would drive down wages for working men. Secondly, women's unions failed female workers because their fees were too high, and union leaders were too middle class. For example, Source 5 argues that women simply did not 'join unions because they were unable or unwilling to pay the necessary dues.' Source 5 argues that this changed during the First World War as women's salaries increased. However, even by 1917, the Agricultural Wages Board agreed a wage of 18 shillings a week for women, compared to 25 shillings for men. The other major problem with women's unions was the presence of middle-class women in leadership who, as Source 6 argues, 'did not always represent what working-class women themselves wanted.' Finally, although as Source 5 highlights, the number of unionised women increased during the First World War, unions failed women at this time. In particular, unions fought for dilution and substitution measures which discriminated against women. Both dilution and substitution downgraded the status of women. The first indicated that one woman could never replace the work done by one man, and the second suggested that women should leave the workforce as soon as men returned from the war. In this way, although there was change over time,

The introduction uses all three sources and recognises that the treatment of women by trade unions changed over time.

This paragraph is structured thematically, presenting three ways in which trade unions failed to support women in the workplace. This helps to organise the information, resulting in a clear argument.

In addition, the paragraph contains a great deal of own knowledge, which is consistently integrated with the sources.

many of the attitudes expressed in Source 4 persisted through to 1918, suggesting that trade unions consistently failed to support women in the workplace between 1875 and 1918.

On the other hand, there were improvements in the way in which trade unions supported women. Source 5 points to the fact that 'improvements in women's salaries by 1914 helped increase the number of women in trade unions.' In fact, in 1906 there were 167,000 women in unions. This increased to 358,000 in 1914, and was accelerated further by the war, reaching 1.2 million by 1918. One way in which female trade union membership increased was through 'the creation of all-female unions' (Source 6). This included the Women's Trade Union League, founded in 1875 by Emma Patterson, the National Federation of Women Workers, founded in 1906. By 1907, the NFWW had 2,000 members, and by 1914, it had 20,000 members. Indeed, the fact that the first women's union was not founded until 1875 partly explains the prejudice expressed in Source 4, a speech given in 1877. Women's trade unions also supported women in the workplace in the sense that they raised awareness of women's rights. Along with suffrage campaigns, this focus on the rights of women led to other unions, such as the National Union of Clerks, allowing men and women to be members on equal terms, and campaigning for equal pay. In this way, trade unions did provide some support for women in the workplace, through all-female unions, and also through mainstream unions which were prepared to fight for equal rights.

In conclusion, trade unions certainly failed to support women at the beginning of the period specified due to prejudice about the role of women, and fear that women would take jobs belonging to men. These attitudes, expressed in Source 4, persisted throughout the First World War and were reflected in the commitment of unions to practices such as substitution and dilution. Even so, as Sources 5 and 6 indicate, there was improvement over time. Greater numbers of women joined unions, and therefore unions became more sensitive to the rights of women.

The own knowledge presented in this paragraph is extremely detailed, as the candidate uses specific figures and accurate dates.

Here, the candidate weighs the evidence presented in Source 4 by noting the date of the source and linking this to the development of the women's trade union movement.

The conclusion uses all three sources to reach an overall judgement that reflects the argument of the essay.

40/40

This essay is strong in terms of own knowledge and the use of the sources. Own knowledge is detailed, precise, accurate and focused. Additionally, the essay is extremely well structured. The candidate has selected information from the sources to support and challenge the view expressed in the question, and gains a mark in Level 4 by weighing the evidence of the sources in paragraph three and in the conclusion.

What makes a good answer?

You have now considered four sample A grade essays. Use these essays to make a bullet-pointed list of the characteristics of an A grade essay. Use this list when planning and writing your own practice exam essays.

Timeline

1832 Great Reform Act

1834 Workhouse Schools created

1839 Custody of Children Act

1850 North London Collegiate School established by Mary Buss

1857 Divorce and Matrimonial Causes Act

1858 Dorothea Beale became Head Mistress of Cheltenham Ladies' College

1867 Women's suffrage first debated in Parliament

Second Reform Act

Agricultural Gangs Act

1869 Municipal Franchise Act

1870 Elementary Education Act

Married Women's Property Act

1872 Girls Public Day School Company established

1873 Custody of Infants Act

Women's Trade Union League founded

1874 Factory Act

1876 The Enabling Act opened all medical colleges to women

1878 Matrimonial Causes Act

Factory and Work Shop Act

1880 Mundella Act

1882 Married Women's Property Act

1883 The Weldon Case

Foundation of the Primrose League

1884 Matrimonial Causes Act

The Third Reform Act

1886 Guardianship of Infants Act

Maintenance of Wives Act

Shop Hours Regulation Act

Foundation of the Women's Liberal Federation

1888 The County Council Act

1891 Factory Act

The Jackson Marriage Case

Elementary Education Act

1894 Local Government Act

1895 Summary Jurisdiction Act (Married Women's Act)

1896 Truck Act

1897 National Union of Women's Suffrage Societies (NUWSS) founded

1901 Factory Act

1902 Education Act (Balfour's Act)

1903 Women's Social and Political Union (WSPU) founded

1906 Foundation of the Women's Labour League

National Federation of Women Workers founded

Education Act (Provision of Meals Act)

1907 Education Act (Administrative Procedures Act)

1910 First Conciliation Bill

Foundation of the National League for Opposing Women's Suffrage

1911 Second Conciliation Bill

Shops Act

1912 Third Conciliation Bill

Franchise Bill

1913 'Cat and Mouse Act' passed

1914 Beginning of the First World War

Queen's Work for Women Fund established

1915 Women's War Register established

1918 Representation of the People Act

1919 Unemployment benefit provided for women

Restoration of Pre-War Practices Act

Repeal of the Sex Disqualification Act

1922 Infanticide Act

Married Women's Maintenance Act

1923 Matrimonial Causes Act

Bastardy Act

1925 The Widows', Orphans, and Old Age Contributory Pensions Act

1928 Equal Franchise Act

Glossary

Age of consent The age at which it is legal to have sexual relations with another person.

Agricultural gangs Groups of farm labourers.

Almroth Wright A scientist notable for his opposition to women's suffrage. He wrote *The Unexpurgated Case Against Woman Suffrage* in 1913.

Amendment A small change to an existing or proposed law.

Anglicans Members of the Church of England.

Arson Illegally and deliberately setting fire to property.

Arthur Balfour A Conservative politician. British Prime Minister between 1902 and 1905.

Autocratic Inflexible and dictatorial leadership by one person, or a small group of people.

Barbara Leigh Smith A campaigner for women's rights in the nineteenth century.

Bestiality Sexual intercourse with an animal.

Bigamy The crime of marrying one person while still being legally married to another.

Bill A proposed law. It becomes an Act once it is formally recognised as a law.

Boer War A conflict between the British Empire and the Dutch free states in South Africa between 1899 and 1902.

Bolshevik Revolution The seizure of power in Russia in 1917 by a Communist group known as the Bolshevik Party.

By-election An election to the House of Commons due to the death or resignation of an existing MP. By-elections happen between General Elections.

Called to the Bar A phrase used to describe somebody who is qualified to act as a barrister in a court of law.

Cat and Mouse Act A slang term for the Prisoners (Temporary Discharge for Ill Health) Act of 1913. The Act allowed the government to release suffragettes on hunger strike, only to re-arrest them as soon as they resumed campaigning.

Census An official survey of the population of a country, collecting data on age, location and occupation.

Charter A document setting out the rights of a person or group.

Coalition Government A government made up of two or more political parties.

Communist A member of the Communist Party. Communists believe that existing society should be replaced by a society in which everyone is equal.

Conciliator A person who aims to reconcile different people or groups with competing interests.

Conjugal rights Rights that partners enjoy as a result of being married to each other, such as the right to live together.

Constituency An area that elects a Member of Parliament.

David Lloyd George Leader of the Liberal Party and British Prime Minister between 1916 and 1922. He was leader of a wartime coalition government during the First World War.

De facto A Latin phrase that means 'about the facts.' It describes the actual nature of a situation.

De jure A Latin phrase that means 'about the law.' It describes the legal nature of a situation.

Decentralised A structure in which power belongs to individuals at a local level rather than being held centrally.

Demobilisation The processes of changing from arrangements necessary for war, to arrangements necessary for peace. This includes discharging troops.

Desertion A situation in which one spouse abandons another for a prolonged period of time.

Direct action A form of protest involving action designed to highlight an inequality.

Dissolved Formally ending a session of Parliament in preparation for a General Election.

Domestic duties Work associated with running a home. This may include looking after children, cooking and cleaning.

Domestic science The study of domestic duties.

Domestic service Paid employment as a servant within a home.

Economic recession A period in which the economy shrinks.

Electoral Advantage The consequence of a reform that changes the electorate in a way that favours one political party.

Emily Davies An advocate for women's education.

Emily Davison A member of the WSPU.

Emmeline Pankhurst The leader of the WSPU. Her daughters Christabel, Sylvia and Adela also played leading roles in the organisation.

Empire A group of countries brought together under the leadership of another country.

Endow To give or bequeath.

Fellow Part of an elite group of learned people who are awarded fellowship to work together as peers in the pursuit of knowledge or practice, often at a university.

Florence Nightingale A nineteenth-century nurse and healthcare reformer.

Franchise The right to vote.

Frederick and Emmeline Pethick-Lawrence Leading campaigners for women's rights. Emmeline was a high-profile member of the WSPU.

Garrison towns Towns with large military populations.

Gender Characteristics of the different sexes.

Godly Exhibiting holy characteristics.

Governesses Women employed to teach children within their own homes.

Gynaecological Relating to the female reproductive system.

Henry Campbell Bannerman Leader of the Liberal Party and British Prime Minister between 1906 and 1908.

Herbert Asquith Leader of the Liberal Party and British Prime Minister between 1908 and 1916.

Higher education University level education.

House of Lords The higher, unelected chamber of the British Parliament.

Householders Homeowners.

Hung Parliament A Parliament in which no Party has a majority.

Hunger strike Refusal to eat as a form of protest.

Infidelity Unfaithfulness to your spouse.

John Bull A fictional figure designed to represent the personification of the British nation.

John Stuart Mill A Liberal politician and philosopher.

Laid off Made redundant.

Law Amendment Society A Society established to campaign for legal equality for men and women.

Liberal A member of the Liberal Party.

Liberal Arts Non-vocational subjects such as History, Literature, Philosophy and Classics.

Lord Chancellor Britain's senior legal officer, responsible for the British justice system.

Lord Curzon A Conservative Lord and outspoken opponent of women's suffrage.

Manifesto A published document outlining a political party's aims and policies.

Manslaughter A legal term which describes the killing of another person. It is distinct from murder in that it is not premeditated and consequently did not carry the death penalty.

Marriage bar The practice of excluding married women from employment. It was justified on the basis that married women should be supported by the income of their husband.

Middle Temple One of four professional bodies that trains and represents barristers.

Militant Aggressive and combative.

Minority government A government which has the support of less than half of the MPs in the House of Commons.

Mrs Humphrey Ward A British novelist and leading member of the anti-suffrage movement.

National elections Elections to the House of Commons.

National Executive Committee The highest committee of the British Labour Party.

National Medical Association A body that represents and regulates medical professionals.

Naval towns Towns with naval garrisons.

Parliamentary candidates People standing for election to Parliament.

Payment in kind Payment in goods rather than money.

Picketing A form of protest in which people gather outside a specific location in which actions are taking place that they oppose.

Post-natal depression Depression following the birth of a child.

Private Member's Bill A Bill introduced to the House of Commons by an individual MP.

Profession A job requiring specialist training. For example, medicine, law and teaching.

Prostitute A person who exchanges sexual favours for money.

Ramsey MacDonald Leader of the Labour Party and British Prime Minister in 1924, and from 1929 to 1935.

Rate-payers People who pay local taxes.

Repeal The removal or reversal of a law.

Satirical A form of humour designed to highlight political inadequacies and social problems.

School Boards Organisations that governed schools.

Secular Not religious.

Shareholders A person or group owning part of a company or organisation.

Shorthand A form of abbreviated note-taking.

Sodomy A legal term meaning an 'unnatural' sexual act. In practice, the term was used to refer to male homosexual acts.

Speaker of the House of Commons The chairperson of the House of Commons.

Speaker's Conference A meeting of senior politicians organised by the Speaker of the House of Commons.

Strike Fund A fund designed to support people who have lost pay through striking.

Suffrage The right to vote.

Telegraph A form of communication in which messages are sent electronically from one place to another.

Trade Union An organisation representing the workers in a specific industry.

Trades Union Congress An organisation representing all British trade unions.

Trojan Horse A term used to describe a gift that conceals an enemy. The term is a reference to an Ancient Greek myth.

Universal suffrage The granting of the vote to all adults.

Velazquez's painting of Venus A sixteenth-century painting of the goddess Venus, owned by the National Gallery.

Victorian period The period covering the reign of Queen Victoria, from 1837 to 1901.

William Gladstone A Liberal politician. Served as British Prime Minister on four occasions; 1868–1874, 1880–1885, February–July 1886 and 1892–1894.

Winston Churchill A Liberal politician and journalist. Later, he joined the Conservative Party and served as Prime Minister from 1940–1945 and 1951–1955.

Women's Land Army An organisation created during the First World War to mobilise women to work on farms.

Workhouse An institution housing those who could not support themselves. Workhouses offered accommodation in return for hard work.

Answers

Section 1: The changing personal status of women

Page 5, Spot the mistake

The paragraph does not get into Level 4 because there is no integration of the sources.

Page 9, Spot the inference

Following the 1878 Matrimonial Causes Act, separations were rare and in many cases beaten women found it hard to obtain a separation. (S)

The Matrimonial Causes Act of 1878 failed to bring about substantial change for women. (I)

Between 1878 and 1893, it was extremely rare for judges to issue separation orders. (P)

The 1878 Matrimonial Causes Act brought about sexual equality for women. (X)

Judges were reluctant to enforce the terms of the 1878 Matrimonial Causes Act. (I)

Page 9, Eliminate irrelevance

There is evidence in all three sources to suggest that legislation between 1873 and 1895 did create a significant change in the legal status of women. Source 3, in reference to the Guardianship of Infants Act of 1886, notes that 'the custom in divorce cases was for custody to go to the innocent parent' suggesting that following divorce mothers and fathers were assessed equally for custody. ~~This source was written Claudia Nelson in 2007 so she was not around at the time she describes~~. Indeed, the Guardianship of Infants Act specifically stated that custody would be granted on the basis of the child's welfare and therefore not according to the gender of the parents. Equally, Source 2 provides an example of a woman being awarded maintenance payments following the 1886 Maintenance of Wives Act. ~~The husband, named Ellis, objected saying that 'his wife had sold his furniture and had really deserted him.'~~ Indeed, the Act stated that wives could receive a maintenance payment of up to £2 per week. In this way, the 1886 Acts clearly improved the status of women because they gave women new legal rights following divorce and separation.

Page 11, Explain the difference: suggested answer

Source 1 suggests that Mrs Jackson is in the wrong and that her husband has been badly treated. Source 2, on the other hand, suggests that the Jacksons' relationship is peaceful, and that Mrs Jackson has treated Mr Jackson well. The difference could be explained by the fact that Source 1 is written by a man, who therefore has a vested interest in asserting the rights of husbands within marriage. Source 2's contrasting account can be explained by the fact that Mrs Jackson was being held captive by her husband when she gave the interview and therefore was not free to give a true account of her feelings about her husband.

Page 11, Write the question: suggested answer

Study Sources 1, 2 and 3.

How far do the sources agree that the actions of Mr Jackson had popular support in 1891?

Page 15, Doing reliability well: suggested answer

Source 1 is unreliable as evidence of public feelings about the Contagious Diseases Act because it comes from *The Shield*, the publication of the Ladies' National Association for the Repeal of the Contagious Diseases Act and therefore contains political bias.

Source 2 is fairly unreliable as evidence of public feelings about the Contagious Diseases Act because it is written by Josephine Butler in her autobiographical work 'Personal Reminiscences of a Great Crusade' and therefore is attempting to protect her reputation as somebody who campaigned on behalf of the public.

Section 2: Women's changing role within the political system, 1870–1920

Page 23, Highlighting integration

Answer 1 is of a higher level.

Page 25, Spot the inference

Only women signed petitions in favour of women's suffrage between 1869 and 1875. (X)

People who supported women's suffrage worked hard to organise petitions and meetings. (P)

Support for women's suffrage increased in the period 1869–1875. (I)

Supporters of women's suffrage used legal means to campaign for the vote. (I)

Supporters of women's suffrage organised larger and larger petitions in favour of the vote. (S)

Page 25, Develop the detail: suggested answer

One reason why women were denied the vote in the period 1869 to 1902 was because they lacked Parliamentary support. Source 2 describes the first

Parliamentary debate on women's suffrage. **The debate was a response to an amendment to the Second Reform Act proposed by the Liberal MP J. S. Mill. Mill's amendment would have given women voting rights on equal terms to men.** It notes that 'the motion was lost, 196 members voting against and 73 for women's suffrage.' In fact, most MPs did not even vote on the issue: **over 400 MPs did not attend the vote.** Source 1 supports this, implying that Parliament refused to respond to an increasing number of petitions in the years 1869 to 1875. **Indeed, Mill's amendment was supported by a petition signed by 1500 men and women and was ignored by the majority of MPs.** Source 3 also indicates that many felt that women lacked 'political knowledge' **as national government was concerned with foreign policy, the empire, and the military, which were considered outside of a woman's sphere of expertise.** Indeed, some politicians argued that women were already represented by the votes of others. **Legally, a vote was given to a household and was cast on behalf of the whole household by the husband or father, who represented their wife and children. A woman's sphere was domestic, and it was believed that women had no interest in political issues.** This is supported by Source 2, in which a Liberal MP suggests women care more about earrings than they do about politics.

Page 27, Doing reliability well: suggested answer

Source 1 is fairly unreliable as evidence of public support for the suffrage movement in 1908 because it is written by a suffragist and may therefore reflect her political bias by exaggerating the level of support for her cause.

Source 2 is reliable as evidence of public support for the suffrage movement in the period 1909–1911 because it is taken from a pamphlet produced by the NUWSS who would have expertise in the sense that they would know how far their organisation had grown between 1909 and 1911.

Page 27, Write the question: suggested answer

Study Sources 1, 2 and 3.

How far do the sources agree that in the period 1908–1911 the NUWSS had significant political influence?

Section 3: Attitudes of politicians, parliament and the public to the suffrage question

Page 39, Spot the mistake

The paragraph does not get into Level 4 because there is no integration of the sources and own knowledge.

Page 39, Spot the inference

To Lloyd George and Churchill, electoral advantage was more important than the principle that women should be allowed to vote. (I)

Most Liberals supported women's suffrage. (X)

Asquith opposed the Second Conciliation Bill. (I)

Lloyd George and Churchill promoted women's suffrage at meetings, but did not support the First Conciliation Bill. (P)

Lloyd George and Churchill supported women's suffrage, but not the Conciliation Bills. (S)

Page 41, Explain the difference: suggested answer

Source 1 suggests that the Election Fighting Fund was an effective alliance between the NUWSS and the Labour Party because it threatened the Conservatives and the Liberals. Source 2, on the other hand, indicates that the alliance between the Labour Party and the NUWSS was problematic because a Labour politician had written a damaging article about women's suffrage. The difference could be explained by the nature of the two sources. Source 1 is a public document produced by the EFF which would be used to persuade the public that the EFF was successful. Source 2 is a private document and therefore has nothing to lose by highlighting tensions in the relationship.

Page 41, Eliminate irrelevance

There is evidence in all three sources that the pact between the NUWSS and the Labour Party was very effective. Source 1 ~~(a pamphlet published by the Election Fighting Fund in 1914)~~ claims that the Election Fighting Fund is 'influencing the vote on which depends the fates of Governments.' There is some evidence for this in the sources. Source 1 claims that the Election Fighting Fund had a significant impact on party politics in Britain. The source states that 'The Liberal Party and the Conservative Party are today threatened by Labour.' This is partly supported by Source 3 ~~(an extract from the annual report of the West Riding branch of the NUWSS, published in 1913)~~ which shows that the NUWSS provided financial support to a Labour candidate in a by-election in 1913. Additionally, Sources 1 and 2 both indicate that the NUWSS had significant influence over the Labour Party. Source 1 states that 'workers will increasingly be associated with the political aims of women', while Source 2 provides evidence of this influence in practice, referring to the NUWSS's success in explaining 'the real situation with regards to women's suffrage' to a member of the Labour Party. ~~Source 2 is taken from the minutes of the Executive Committee of the Election Fighting Fund, 6 December 1912.~~

Page 43, Write the question: suggested answer

Use Sources 1, 2 and 3 and your own knowledge.

Do you agree with the view that the trade union movement failed to support the extension of the franchise to women in the period 1884–1914?

Page 47, Doing reliability well: suggested answer

Source 1 is unreliable as evidence of public feelings about the Representation of the People Act of 1918 because Isabella Ford is writing to the NUWSS magazine and therefore the letter reflects the political bias of the author and the magazine, rather than the feelings of the public.

Source 2 is unreliable as evidence of public feelings about the Representation of the People Act of 1918 because it is a speech by Herbert Asquith in 1920 and therefore it reflects Asquith's political bias (that is to say, his antipathy to women getting the vote). In addition, it is an attempt by Asquith to defend his reputation in the sense that he had opposed women's suffrage whilst Prime Minister and, in 1920, following the passage of the Representation of the People Act, he was keen to justify his opposition.

Source 3 is reliable as evidence of public feelings about the Representation of the People Act of 1918 because it is written by historians and therefore draws on their expertise.

Section 4: Changing educational and employment opportunities for women 1870–1930

Page 53, Spot the inference

Hilda Martindale's mother was unable to establish a girls' school in Lewes so she moved to Brighton, where there was a girls' school. (S)

Attitudes to the education of girls differed from place to place. (I)

The girls' school in Brighton had met with no opposition. (X)

People in Lewes were conservative in their social and religious outlook. (P)

Education provision for girls differed from place to place. (I)

Page 55, Write the question: suggested answer

Use Sources 1, 2 and 3 and your own knowledge.

Do you agree with the view that Dorothea Beale and Frances Mary Buss fundamentally changed attitudes to the education of girls in the period 1860–1910?

Page 61, Eliminate irrelevance

There is evidence in all three sources that suggests that trade unions did, as Source 3 claims, 'a great favour to the cause of the woman worker.' ~~All three sources were written between 1875 and 1925, a period when many women were joining unions.~~ Sources 1, 2 and 3 agree that women are exploited by employers. Source 1 claims that 'women need protection', while Source 2 refers to women workers paid on '8 shillings a week.' Similarly, Source 3 objects to 'starvation wages and intolerable conditions'. All three sources make these statements to underline the benefits for women of joining a union. Sources 2 and 3 provide evidence of the support provided by unions. ~~Source 3 was written after Source 2.~~ Source 2 contrasts wages of unionised and non-unionised women, claiming that unionised women earn '30 shillings a week'. Similarly, Source 3 argues that 'the strike among women employed at Millwall Food Preserving Factory would have been doomed to failure' without the support of the National Federation of Women Workers. ~~The National Federation of Women Workers was founded in 1906, and by 1907 it had 2,000 members.~~

Page 61, Doing reliability well: suggested answer

Source 1 is unreliable as a description of public attitudes to the unionisation of women because it reflects George Howell's vested interest in boosting the membership, and therefore the power, of his trade union.

Source 2 is unreliable as a description of the impact of the unionisation of women because it is based on a second-hand account. The author of the source is reporting Mr W. C. A. Andersons' account of the good work done by unions, but the author is not a witness of this work itself.

Page 63, Explain the difference: suggested answer

Source 1 argues that women are working extremely effectively in factories. In contrast, Source 2 indicates that women's work is limited in comparison to the work of men and boys. The difference could be explained by the fact that Source 1 is published in 1916 and Source 2 is published in 1919. Source 1 may present a more positive view of women's work because in 1916 women were still relatively newly employed in war industries and so there was limited data available on their impact. In addition, the government needed to encourage employers to employ more women in industry. By 1919, detailed data was available on the impact of women in war work and there was a perceived need to ensure that employers employed men returning from the war.

Page 63, Write the question: suggested answer

Study Sources 1, 2 and 3.

How far does the evidence of Sources 1, 2 and 3 agree with the view that women's work during the First World War was responsible for 'breaking up old superstitions' regarding the ability of women in the workplace?